# THE CONFIDENT PERFORMER

*Rethinking Mental Performance for Athletes, Coaches, and Parents*

ANDREA WIELAND, PH. D., M.B.A., OLY

Self-published in the United States of America.

ISBN: 979-8-89694-610-6 - Ebook
ISBN: 979-8-89694-611-3 - Paperback
ISBN: 979-8-89694-628-1 - Hardcover

LCCN: 2025913787

Cover Design: TJ Marquis

First Edition

# Dedication

To my parents, William F. and Aileen W. Wieland, and my immediate and extended family: You held high expectations, exemplified excellence, and provided the support, genetics, inspiration, and competitive standards for high achievement.

To my friends, partners, and teammates for life from Westtown, Iowa, US Field Hockey, and beyond: Thank you for the love, laughs, tears, and for having my back and allowing me to have yours.

To my coaches, teachers, professors, supervisors, and colleagues at Westtown, Iowa, ICPH, 7th Group, IMG Academy, UPenn, Sensei-Porcupine Creek, and USAFA: You made me a better leader, team member, and contributor.

Finally, to my furry companions: Your unconditional love and consistency kept me connected to nature and to all the beauty that beautiful Planet Earth has to offer.

You helped me get through the struggle and stay connected to the bigger picture of life.

# Contents

# Introduction

If you're an athletic director or an executive director of a sports club, you're likely very familiar with both the thrill of a roaring crowd and the gripping tension of silence in a budget meeting. As a warrior of managing various responsibilities, navigating the stormy seas of complaints and compliance, budget cuts and shortages, and the ever-present worries about ensuring the safety, protection, and well-being of student-athletes can feel heavy and draining.

Complaints about coaches, communication concerns, and attracting and retaining high-quality athletic staff are ever-present boulders to climb. With all these challenges, the risk of burnout for longtime athletic directors is high, as the reward may not be worth the challenges. Then add in concerns about how to best manage the mental health and welfare of student-athletes, which is ever present in the minds of every leader, coach, and parent. Yet despite it all, watching student-athletes and coaches thrive and experience the thrill of competition can motivate you to persevere.

This book emphasizes the joy of the meaningful moments that attracted you to this fulfilling career. It is also intended to be your beacon of guidance, equipping you with the practical strategies, skills, and framework that you need to navigate your challenges with grace and confidence, so you can offer that same grace, poise, and confidence to the parents, athletes, and coaches you work with. You hold the guardianship of your coaches and athletes' most precious lifelong dreams and goals, and their potential to do great things in the world as future leaders. Your legacy matters.

So make the most of it, using the guidance offered in this book to more meaningfully impact the lives of student-athletes, coaches, and parents in the ways you'd envisioned. This blueprint of lifelong confidence that you now hold in your hands will help you rediscover the joy in your role, lead with the clarity and confidence that makes every day more fun and rewarding, and ease the restlessness of a stressed mind and heart. If you're a motivated performer, this book will help guide you to achieving new heights of mental fortitude.

I'm no stranger to the pressures you face and the unique challenges that raise the stress levels of athletic directors and sports executives. As your guide, I draw on my depth of experience from my Olympic journey and in coaching top achievers as a performance psychologist. My greatest life reward is coaching motivated individuals to improve and supporting good performers into becoming great ones. My job is to help others win by teaching them to embody the mindset and skills to show up confidently and thrive under intense pressure.

This book distills my lifelong adventures of finding, using, and teaching the most optimal, practical, and scientifically backed strategies for leading individuals and teams to consistently outperform their limits. Throughout my career, I have helped professional athletes, elite high school and collegiate athletes, Special Ops soldiers, and high-profile business leaders to improve their game of achieving self-mastery and increasing their confidence despite high-pressure stakes and challenges. I have delved deep into the characteristics, mindsets, and skills of some of the greatest warriors on the planet, which I will share with you here. My personal and professional experiences center on navigating the difficulties of competitive athletics. As a coach, practitioner, administrator, and former Olympic field hockey athlete, I have tasted the bitter pangs of defeat and experienced the thrill of last-second victories. These types of experiences deeply affect the hearts and minds of those who prepare themselves for their most significant moments and have personally impacted me well beyond the scoreboard.

Imagine your teams, coaches, athletes, staff, and parents all showing up as the best versions of themselves and making the intentional choice of self-mastery in their victory call. The secret sauce of championship teams and that of people learning to champion their lives is composed of intense trust, confidence, ownership of their choices, and accountability to those around them. It takes a systems approach to succeed in self-mastery. Trust is the key to not just surviving but thriving. The competitive arena becomes a spiritual training ground for building intense trust in oneself and others through self-mastery. Winning more games is excellent, but winning in life is the most remarkable outcome of this journey.

In this book, you will embark on a transformative adventure that starts with deeply examining four primary sources of your identity. Knowing who you are is foundational in crafting intentional personas that align with your greatest aspirations. We will dive deep into understanding yourself as a whole person and as a healthy and confident performer. You will learn how to eliminate unnecessary suffering, forge resilience, cultivate anti-fragile confidence, and integrate permanent well-being into your peak performance through repetition, iterations, and curious reflections. You will learn to adapt and excel with the poise of the most coveted GOATs (greatest of all time) and become the champion you have always strived to be.

## What Wins

Jax turned to me and said, "I love this job. It's just the people who make it so difficult!" She smiled jokingly, shrugged her shoulders, and turned toward the conference room. "By the way, thank you for your parenting presentation on Wednesday. The parents flooded my inbox with great feedback from their experience. Many discovered some new points of self-awareness and connected to what they can bring to the Champions' Culture we are creating here. Gotta start this next meeting. Now, it's time to 'breathe and have fun,' as you like to say!"

"Let's go, Jax! You've got this," I replied. We high-fived playfully, and Jax entered her sponsorship strategy meeting with the marketing team to secure next year's funding. Like many top Division I athletic directors and executive directors of large sports organizations, Jax Daytona wears several hats. One of her most important responsibilities is ensuring the positive sporting experiences of student-athletes, coaches, staff, parents, and spectators.

Part of that means hiring extraordinary people to give the athletic departments a "leg up" in creating wins. Winning alone is not what makes sports enjoyable; however, winning is fun and the experience of victory should extend beyond the scoreboard. People want to be a part of and get behind a winning team. When teams, coaches, and athletes win and have great experiences, an athletic director's or sports executive's job becomes easier, with fewer tensions and less blaming, shaming, and complaining from all levels.

You might guess that the key to winning more consistently would involve having more money, better facilities, more significant sponsorships, larger donations, better athletes, winning coaches, and/or more substantial and experienced staff. However, confidence is the foundational secret sauce to achieving all of those material wins. Confidence, or lack thereof, pervades all aspects of every sports organization. The feeling of confidence does not randomly come out of the blue or fall from the sky. It comes from doing the work with others; preparing well; developing trust in yourself, your teammates, and the system; and securing a belief that you have earned the right to perform well today.

We all want to own our confidence, have a stronger sense of self, and feel more secure and comfortable in our skin in various situations, whether they involve new people, new teammates or coaches, longtime friends, or family. We all want to become who we are meant to be and achieve our goals and intentions, and who doesn't enjoy the fun of winning? It may seem though that the feeling of confidence can be elusive, unpredictable, and inconsistently attainable. Everybody wants to have more confidence, yet particularly in situations involving competition, external forces can make it feel difficult to consistently access it.

Winning is far more than what the results reflect; it is a deeply personal experience. It is about knowing who you are, who you are meant to be, and who you intend to be in the world. Winning happens when everyone knows their roles and responsibilities and understands their common goal. It requires a system of parents, athletes, coaches, and the Team Around the Team (TAT) members all being on the same page. The system makes a commitment to help bring forth the best in themselves and each other. As in the acronym PACT, which stands for parents, athletes, coaches, and TAT, everyone matters and plays a vital role in the success of a winning system.

We are teleological, or goal-oriented beings. Even so-called "non-competitive" people set goals and intentions, consciously or not. Since you're reading this book about confidence, winning, and enhancing performance, you're likely a competitive person who wants to win and feel good about yourself while pursuing your most challenging goals. Whether your goals are granted, given, or self-imposed, let's go for the win! I am here to help you find a better way. I wrote this book to help us all win more, to guide you in how to play better and win at the winnable game of confidence ownership.

Sports and other highly competitive environments, such as music, the military, the arts, and business settings, provide outstanding playing grounds for building confidence, developing trust, testing skills, setting and achieving challenging goals, and learning to team up and work well with others. It's the ultimate training ground for learning how to win the Game of consistent confidence known as self-mastery, or what I call confidence ownership.

Regardless of the performance arena, we all want to rely on ourselves and others and feel confident that things will work out and that people will do what they say they will. We want to relax with a sense of safety and know that everything will be okay, and be ourselves and feel that we belong. Magical things happen with the fairy dust of trust. Achieving trust and thereby greater confidence may not seem so hard when put so simply.

## My Experience

I have worn many of the shoes and hats that you are now wearing. Growing up in a highly competitive academic and athletic family, being a high performer academically and athletically was not only encouraged but also expected. I was surrounded by cousins who were great athletes and attended the most competitive top universities in the USA, including Division I schools such as Stanford, Yale, Harvard, Duke, Princeton, Brown, William and Mary, and Bucknell. My step-grandfather, George Munger, had been the head football coach at the University of Pennsylvania (UPenn) during their glory years.

Needless to say, I grew up with overly inflated aspirations to be an Olympic athlete, having no idea that it would take 21 years to achieve that feat. I wanted to change the world through the field of psychology by supporting and coaching people to be their best selves. My father was a psychiatrist, and I wanted to be like him. He was highly intelligent, with a calm, soothing presence and a gentle sense of humor, and was skilled at articulating just the right words to ease challenging situations. When he returned home from work, I sprinted out the door to greet him, carry his briefcase, and ask about his day. We discussed his engaging patients, although he always maintained confidentiality, and I loved learning about the human psyche. When I was in the fifth and sixth grades, my mother, Aileen, was earning her second master's degree, this time in counseling psychology. I became the client she targeted in her counseling skills practice, and, disrespectfully, I gave her plenty of eye rolls, heavy sighs, and walkouts since I was not interested in naming my emotions and telling her how I felt. Psychology lived in our family milieu.

In most circumstances, I naturally take the reins and lead my friends and peers. After my dad established an emotional wellness center in the mid-80s, I envisioned leading some type of human performance center with him in the future. I jokingly said that Wieland and Wieland would be on the door with my name listed first. I failed in pursuing my early dreams, but sports helped me learn how to get up and persist after losses and regain my confidence. Now, I use sports systems to educate parents, athletes, and coaches on developing sustainable confidence in all areas of their lives.

## My start in mental training

One day when my sister and I were playing tennis with some friends, fate decided my sporting and professional career. On that day in particular, my insatiable demands of myself to deliver high performance and my harsh self-criticisms of mistakes made for an accelerated downward spiral of poor play. The more I tightened up with my expectations and reactions to mistakes, the worse I played. Countless eye rolls, terrible body language, and barking at myself all came to a head, and I turned to the cement wall that supported the structure of the court, and—WHAM!—cracked my racket frame against the wall with the force and repetition of a lumberjack and axe felling a tree. The frame crumpled like an aluminum can being crushed, leaving me with no racket and plenty of time to pout.

The destroyed racket ratted out my intense, unmanaged emotions on the court. What was supposed to be a friendly, fun, lightly competitive game with friends turned into a disproportionate temper tantrum. My sister only rolled her eyes. She and her friends continued to play as I sulked away from around the court. I would have to tell my parents what had happened and face their disappointment.

Moreover, I now had to face Guy Rhodes. He heard my outburst, which had reverberated across the lake, and came out to see what was happening. I was violating his ground rules of having fun and respecting the game of tennis. He came out sporting a very old, faded, and well-loved red T-shirt that read "Aw Doo-Doo" in simple white letters across the front. Undoubtedly, one of his tennis buddies had screen printed it for him. "Aw Doo-Doo" was his signature saying upon missing a shot or when someone else missed theirs.

When anyone made a mistake on the tennis court, he would smile and gently say, "Aw Doo-Doo," with the playful and serene nature of a Buddha. All who heard it were reminded to stay light-hearted and not take themselves or the game of tennis too seriously. Chuckles and laughter from everyone left people smiling with their hearts feeling whole, as a reminder that tennis is supposed to be fun.

Guy Rhodes approached when he saw me slumped and sulking in the courtside folding chair. "Andrea, would you like a sandwich?" I looked up at him with teary eyes, feeling disappointed in myself. I was embarrassed that I had behaved so poorly and violated the straightforward rules of using his court. "What is the matter with me?" I thought, "How do I lack the maturity or self-control to follow these ever-so-simple rules?" Granted, I was around 10 years old, but I did know better. "Do better when you know better," I muttered to myself.

I said, "Sure. Thank you" and followed him into the house he had built. He remained quiet as he made a ham and cheese sandwich on white bread with some chips on the side. He slid the plate to me and sat beside me on the adjacent bar stool at the kitchen countertop. I could hear my sister and her friends laughing and having a good time on the tennis court while I braced myself for the scolding I rightfully deserved.

"It sounded like you were having a hard time out there," Guy started gently, probingly.

"Yes, I'm so sorry, Guy. I know I broke your rules, and I was getting so mad at myself that I was playing so badly."

"Yes, I heard. I think the whole lake heard." He paused, letting the gravity of his words sink in. "The whole reason I built that court was for people to enjoy a wonderful game together, to be social, meet new people, and for young and old to socialize in a relaxed, beautiful setting. So, allowing yourself to get so mad does not promote the whole reason for building the court." He paused as tears began to well up in my eyes.

"I know you can do it because I have seen you having fun. You are such a nice young player. So much talent and athleticism. We do not want to waste our abilities because we cannot control our emotions and forget to have fun. Now, I will ask you not to play here for two weeks to help you remember that we are here to have fun on the court. I will remind you what you can say when you make a mistake or when things are not going your way." He pointed to his shirt and underlined the words with his finger: "Aw doo-doo." I smiled, wiped my tears, finished my chips, and thanked him for the sandwich. I apologized a second time and let him know that it would not happen again. And it didn't.

When we returned to Atlanta, my mother gave me a book called *The Inner Game of Tennis* by Tim Galwey and a new tennis racket, to which I had to contribute my small allowance and chore money to help pay for. Galwey's book, popularized in the 1970s, was my first introduction to self-help and mental training books. It remains a mental game classic today that I highly recommend. I devoured it in a day because I easily related to its message, and it ignited my passion for reading books about mental toughness and training. My love-love journey with the mental Game started with a tantrum and has now flourished into a career.

In this book, I will share what I have learned from my experiences, what the literature tells us from research studies, and what I gained from leading other practitioners in delivering a holistic 360-degree model to elite athletes from high school students to pros. I have tested out all of my advice on myself and thousands of others over three decades of delivering products, services, and consultations in high-performance spaces.

My company, Winning System Psychology, PC, has a soul and sole mission to develop as many champions of self-mastery as possible. Self-mastery champions have clarified who they are and the game they are playing and can maintain a stable sense of joy and confidence despite the people, pressures, or circumstances they are dealing with. They are the kind of people the human species so desperately needs at this juncture in history. Becoming a self-mastery champion is exponentially more possible when you surround yourself with others who are also pursuing this goal and investing in owning their confidence.

## What You Can Expect from This Book

Section 1 focuses on knowing and playing the ultimate life game, the right Game of self-mastery as your source of consistent confidence, no matter the arena or the pressures encountered. Learning to play the right Game allows you to become a force for good. It's the "game changer" you've been looking for. It's always been available to you, but shifts in your thinking are required to successfully play the Game and achieve life's ultimate rewards. I will clarify the rules of the Game, the players, their roles, and their responsibilities, so you and the entire system can play to win.

Section 2 is all about strategy. You will learn the Confident Performer model to understand why building a solid foundation as a human first is required for sustainable confidence across multiple domains, sustainable mental health, optimal performance, and a lifetime of confidence. The blueprint provides an ever-evolving approach to deeply knowing and embracing your Human-First identities. As you evolve, the blueprint will evolve with you.

Section 3 offers the theory of multiple selves in place of a unified personality theory, discussing four primary sources of identity at the intersection of nature, nurture, and affiliation. This information will empower you to make conscious choices about who you want to be today and in the future based on your primary goals.

Section 4 examines who you must become in your chosen identities to reach your most important goals. You will be encouraged to align your virtues, values, and targeted behaviors with your chosen identities. We will also examine your superpowers and kryptonite to ensure you can set yourself up for daily success and small wins on your way to the big wins.

Section 5 aims to help you commit to the six fundamentals of a whole person and a healthy performer. You will be more ready to bounce back or even forward from setbacks and prevent, reduce, or mitigate the chances of mental and physical injury or illness.

Section 6 focuses on mindsets, strategies, and skills needed to enjoy performing under various circumstances with diverse people and under intense pressure with confidence, fun, and composure. We will look at the core mental skills needed to build deliberate, high-quality practices with mindsets that serve your performance, health, and growth as a high achiever.

Section 7 looks at how all this fits into helping others win and being a force for good. You can benefit from the process of self-mastery while raising the level of performance of the systems you play a part in, and learn to win because of your struggles as you forge anti-fragile confidence. Finally, you will reflect on what is immediately implementable.

Whether you identify as a parent, coach, athlete, or member of the TAT, your self-mastery adventure starts with deciding to play a new Game. When practiced and referred to consistently over time, the blueprint provided in this book will pave the way toward a life well-lived, and humanity will benefit from your contributions. May you be inspired to take consistent action that builds momentum. Owning your confidence promises to deliver the joy, poise, freedom, and consistent self-mastery you have always wanted.

## Do the Work

Perhaps like me, you have read many personal development books in search of golden nuggets of truth with the hope that your life would change for the better once you acquired them, but you have just found similar truth bombs repeated in different ways. The difference in this book is that I will wholeheartedly encourage you to move from intellectualizing the information to practicing the concepts, tools, and skills consistently so you can master them. When used and wielded, these tools will help you build intense trust in yourself and enable other people to trust you more.

Please act quickly on the ideas that resonate with you. As Dr. Phil Stutz, psychiatrist and coach to the stars, says, "Speed is a force." The faster you act and put the ideas into play, the quicker you will gain experiences, make them your own, and achieve more control over your performance. Your relationships will improve, and you will find more joy in your sport. Waiting to get started delays motivation and decays momentum.

With that said, not every tool will work for you. Elizabeth Ricker, an author, researcher, and scientist, popularized neuro-hacks in her book, *Smarter Tomorrow*. She recognizes that brains are so unique that a neuro-hack or self-experiment for one brain may or may not work for another. I often recommend the concept of scientific self-help to people I work with and encourage them to test it for themselves. A one-time attempt at practicing a skill or tool I offer here will likely not create much change, so I encourage giving each new concept at least several chances. As with any physical skill, learning new ideas takes time and repetition to figure out how they will work best for you. There will be certain processes, concepts, and techniques that will resonate with you, and others that won't cut it. As you progress, you may try one of the skills later and find that it works when you are more ready.

In some cases, you may notice more immediate effects. For example, when you first try breathing exercises for performance, such as nasal breathing, you may experience immediate benefits. Typically, people feel calmer, more clear-headed, and more energized after practicing new breathing techniques even the first time.

Practicing other skills such as self-talk or shifting your body language can also have an immediate effect when practiced just once. Try it now: Breathe in and out smoothly with your chest up, shoulders back, chin level, and sitting up tall. Did anything change after one to three rounds of breath? Do you feel more alert and slightly more energized? Like any skill or tool, the skills offered here have subtler applications that will require practice to become automatic when needed.

I encourage you to practice each tool several times until you know it. Then, try it in a variety of situations. If you find no progress, don't like it, or do not think the tool works for you, there is no need to add it to your toolbox. If you find your proverbial toolbox taking on too much clutter and causing more confusion than benefit, put a few tools aside and focus on what works for you. Enjoy the process of testing, modifying, adding, and deleting. Here's to achieving your highest and best selves and to your self-mastery adventure!

# SECTION 1

## Getting Right with Yourself First

# Chapter 1

# The Ultimate Game

The Game of confidence ownership is not new and has been studied since ancient times. The Greco-Roman Stoic philosophers called it self-mastery and touted it as being the path to living a meaningful life that is intrinsically and extrinsically rewarding. I call it confidence ownership but will use these terms interchangeably throughout this book.

Owning your confidence involves doing what you can do with poise, belief, and trust that things will work out. You may be in an entirely new situation without having built the necessary skills to effectively navigate it, but you can still demonstrate confidence in your openness to learning and asking questions as you work to gain greater competency with specific skills.

This can be easier said than done, especially when things aren't going well, yet that is when self-mastery matters most. It's easy to be in control of yourself when everything is going your way. When external pressure weighs on you, that's the perfect time to lean on your mental training. I will show you how. Whenever you recognize a chaotic moment as being an opportunity to learn and grow, you are winning the inner Game of self-mastery. You cannot spell "winner" without "inner." And here we are talking about winning your inner game first.

Self-mastery enables you to take an empowered response instead of a reactive one. Adverse reactions, such as overly aggressive or defensive responses, are often caused by feeling controlled or threatened by people, events, or circumstances. In the Game of confidence ownership, you don't solely rely on others to pat you on the back and tell you everything will be okay. Although encouragement is one of the greatest gifts you can receive, if you constantly rely on other people to help you feel better, you may be disappointed when someone does not adequately support you, or support does not come in the packaging you prefer.

When you are in the response mode, you are in control of yourself, recognizing that most circumstances are outside of your control. Thus, the Game of confidence ownership involves training yourself to operate from a place where you can respond as effectively as possible, which is an important skill for getting you closer to achieving what you want. Reacting to and focusing on what others are saying or doing will not get you closer to regulating yourself. We cannot control others. We can only control our responses. Instead, aim your focus on being the better best version of yourself.

The challenge is when we're not taught the Game of self-mastery, then we're likely in a reactive mode, causing unnecessary harm to ourselves and others when situations are uncomfortable or chaotic. Let's examine one of the most reactive and destructive dynamics in unhealthy relationships: the drama triangle. Dr. Stephen Karpman, a psychiatrist who studied dysfunctional social dynamics related to power differentials, first proposed this concept.[1] Increasing your understanding of how the drama triangle works can empower you to decide not to play a part.

The drama triangle describes the unconscious dynamic wherein two people get pulled into playing one of three roles: victim, perpetrator, and/or rescuer. When conflict erupts into fights, person A may become the victim, and person B becomes the perpetrator. Another scenario might be that person B becomes the victim and person A assumes the rescuer role. In any scenario, neither person is aware that they are playing these roles; they are "unconscious" of the familiar dynamic they are being drawn into playing. The roles are not static, however, and sometimes a victim in one scenario becomes the rescuer or perpetrator in another.

The rescuer is driven by guilt to offer help and maintains the victim's dependency and alliance so that the rescuer can feel as if they have power. A rescuer's offer of help tends to perpetuate the victim's dependency because the rescuer relies on their ability to provide help for their personal sense of self-worth. The perpetrator blames and attacks the victim and doesn't have to take responsibility or accountability for their actions and words. The perpetrator fears not being good enough and tries to avoid having to see themselves that way by blaming others for the perpetrator's own shortcomings.

A person with unhealthy boundaries may play one role more often than another. The drama triangle is an unconscious dynamic where someone may play all three roles, even with the same conflict or repeated fight, until a more mature decision is made not to continue playing out this dynamic. For example, person A, the victim, may become the perpetrator when they try to stand up for themselves. Person B, who was the perpetrator, then becomes the victim, which triggers Person C to now become the rescuer.

Later in Section 3, Chapter 10, we will also examine the role of Saboteurs as being part of your whole self. Saboteurs, victims, perpetrators, and rescuers all have positive intentions but are lousy at effectively helping others because they are stuck in a time when they were unable to respond maturely. This book will teach you how to get to know your internal parts through the Internal Family Systems Model (Schwartz 1985), understand their positive intentions, and help them agree to play other roles. In your new Game of self-mastery, you will consciously become the leader of your parts.

Understanding the drama triangle and the impacts of your own Saboteurs is critical for discussing identities, roles, and goals, and creating winning systems. The drama triangle often plays out in teams and families between coaches and players, athletes and parents, and parents and coaches. Let's learn to play a better game by mastering ourselves first. Winning the game of self-mastery requires consciously deciding to not play a role in the drama triangle and instead take accountability for your own actions.

## The Promise of Confidence Ownership

Joy arises from leading yourself well, working well with others, and leading others effectively through exemplary actions. The Buddha said it best: "It is better to conquer yourself than to win a thousand battles. Then the victory is yours. It cannot be taken from you by angels, demons, heaven, or hell." Indeed, winning external battles can be satisfying, but they pale in comparison to winning internal battles. Mastering your mind and emotions allows your spirit to be enduringly indomitable.

Additionally, self-mastery provides a sense of discernment for knowing when to lead and when to follow. Accept and embrace that part of every human's experience is that hiccups, wrongdoings, and disappointments are inevitable! It is not a matter of whether something will go wrong along your journey, but when. When you face seemingly insurmountable obstacles or challenges, self-mastery will give you the skills to bounce forward and endure the most harrowing moments. You will learn, grow, and become stronger because of the adversity, not despite it. Developing a support system that you grow and nurture over time can be invaluable as well. Owning your confidence is about staying focused on and enjoying the unfolding process of learning and growth. With the right attitude, every opportunity and challenge can become an opportunity for growth. Every inner win is a victory for, and because of, self-mastery.

On the other hand, when you believe "I am only valuable if I play well. My self-worth is dependent on me playing well," then you're playing the wrong game. When you play or compete poorly, which is inevitable at some point during your career, it does not make you less valuable of a person; it simply means that you did not play well that day. When the game or competition is over, take the learning experience as a win, glean the lessons, and move on.

Kristin Neff's research on self-compassion tells us that playing the shame game and beating yourself up for poor performance are not sustainable strategies for self-improvement. I'm not suggesting that you drop your standards and aim for mediocrity, but cultivating self-compassion provides the space, grace, and motivation to work on changes instead of wasting time and energy on negativity. This will be discussed more in depth in upcoming chapters.

Confidence ownership helps you rely on yourself and not take things so personally, empowering you to accept feedback and suggestions for improvement without thinking you are a terrible person for not being perfect. This practice helps you recover from setbacks and mistakes, knowing they are not the end of the world, and also allows you to give the best of what you have in various situations. Your willingness to learn, grow, and be curious allows you to maintain your sense of self regardless of your level of competence at a skill or task.

Owning your confidence gives you the courage to do hard things while bridging the divide between where you are now and where you are headed. I promise you that attaining greater self-mastery will bring you sustainable happiness and satisfaction in sports and life. You will be able to achieve your most important and challenging goals while surviving and thriving through any demoralizing setbacks.

## The False Promise

Media advertising in our society has sold us on the idea that the right game to play in pursuing happiness is about achieving external results and consuming products. Grand achievements, such as getting into a prestigious school or college, having a cool car or beautiful house, making a lot of money, or popularity on social media all seem sexy. The misconception is that achieving those experiences will sustain happiness, contentment, and a sense of freedom and enjoyment in the long run.

Unfortunately, research repeatedly shows that these achievements, without the underpinnings of character development and an inner sense of self, give false promises of lifelong happiness, contentment, and inner peace. Without self-mastery, these empty promises lead to feelings of short-term pleasure from a quick hit of dopamine and the temporary high of getting something new. The short-term, powerful high results in longer-term feelings of emptiness and discontentment when that high wears off. When we don't get what we want, including a long-term sense of joy, mastery, and confidence, we feel like victims or that life is unfair.

I have met and worked with many ultra-wealthy people—who externally appear to be the elite of the most successful—who are unhappy, discontented, and feel trapped in their lives. Materialistic lifestyles don't seem to bring people lasting happiness. Without an internal compass that guides you, a solid sense of who you are, and a strong sense of what matters to you most and how you want to show up consistently and confidently, the chasing of external wins will persist without the satisfaction that comes when the wins are achieved. When you are miserable with yourself, it is impossible to feel a sense of accomplishment, no matter how grand your accomplishments are. As will be discussed further in chapter 10, the "never enough" Saboteur takes over and wreaks havoc on sustainable happiness.

A person playing the wrong game thinks they must constantly set up the next significant external achievement, hoping it will bring them lifelong contentment. I was once one of those people. I fell into the trap of pursuing the next grand achievement—including earning a PhD and MBA, competing in the Olympics, succeeding at business ownership, and earning position titles at world-renowned brands—in desperate pursuit of gaining approval, adoration, and affection from others. I soon discovered though that these achievements did not lead to sustainable happiness when I lacked self-mastery and trust in myself.

Even competing in the Olympics, which was my lifelong pursuit from ages 6 to 27, did not offer me the glory I sought. Little did I realize that the glory I needed could only come from self-acceptance and self-approval. Without a more complete sense of self and a desperate need for external validation, even making it to the Olympics could not fill that sense of lack or resolve the "not good enough" feelings I harbored deep in my bones. You can achieve considerable success through self-mastery, enhanced life satisfaction, and sustained happiness through confident ownership. In this book, we will examine the other games people play that get in the way of realizing their best selves and biggest goals.

## Overly Focused on Outcomes

The comparison game can either motivate those who see what's possible or demoralize those who see how far they need to go. Those who overly focus on the outcomes of others compared to their own results tend to suffer and feel as if their own lives are lacking. Negatively comparing yourself to others when you are two different humans makes little sense. Yet, without self-mastery, it's done all the time.

Which is better, an apple or an orange? Neither. Because they are different, one cannot compare them. Preferences make one better for one person and the other better for another. And still others don't even like fruit.

Like I encourage my clients, I encourage you to compare your process with others, not compare results. Compare your processes with those you deem "better than you." What is the person doing that is part of their formula for success and well-being? Do you have the complete picture?

Observe to learn. Ask the person about their consistent practices that serve them well. Most will be flattered that you asked if you have sincere curiosity. You can always "beg, borrow, or mimic" what others do well to see what may work for you. As infants and children, we mimicked to learn.

Another helpful side to comparing is when it helps you see what's possible and motivates you, not defeats you. For example, When I was a freshman in college, I looked up at the wall of photographs of All-America athletes that were hanging in the University of Iowa field hockey locker room and promised myself I would be on that wall too. I had no jealousy because I was not collegiate-level All-America material yet, but I knew I could get there with the right work ethic, commitment, and attitude. "If they can do it, I could do it," I thought to myself, not knowing I was using one of Albert Bandura's sources of self-efficacy: Vicarious learning. Vicarious learning is a useful comparison to others. Let's take a look at one of the best examples of vicarious learning.

A famous example of vicarious learning involves breaking the four-minute mile barrier, which was first accomplished by Sir Roger Bannister in 1954 with a time of 3 minutes, 59.4 seconds. Before Roger's incredible feat, scientists had deemed that running a mile in under four minutes was impossible. Amazingly, once it was done, others' beliefs about what was possible then changed! The feat was accomplished again only two months after Bannister showed it was possible. As of June 2022, almost 1,800 athletes have broken the four-minute mile. Following this example, I encourage you to use social comparison to examine great performers' processes. Success leaves clues! The comparison game thus becomes a way of learning and adapting from others' successes while you test out what works for you in pursuing your highest aspirations.

Comparing yourself to others in a healthy way is useful when you can learn from someone else's process. Consider examining any unhealthy comparisons you may have. Ask, "Are my comparisons to others healthy or unhealthy? Are they inspiring me to pursue new opportunities, or hurting me by increasing my self-criticism and limiting beliefs?"

Many high achievers fear losing their edge or motivation if they are not hard on themselves, don't compare themselves to others, or grind themselves down with criticism. What if you, instead, compare yourself to your own improvement over time and set up deliberate practices? When you are deliberate about your improvement and compare your process with the processes of those who are achieving the same goals you want to achieve, you give yourself the chance to maintain your confidence while you grow and learn.

Finally, the game of outcomes focuses on the idea that "you will arrive." Have you ever thought that once you achieve a certain goal, you will then be forever happy, worthy, and anointed as a success in the eyes of others? Is it only upon achieving your wildly important goal that you can be happy? My greatest dream of becoming an Olympian took 21 years to accomplish, with much disappointment and hardship along the way. The anticipation of finally being named to the US National Field Hockey team had been building in me for decades. I promised myself that when I finally "made it," I would feel elated and have the approval, admiration, and respect of others for the rest of my life. But when I finally made it to the 1994 World Cup in Dublin, Ireland, I looked around for the metaphorical parade, fireworks, and balloons. Hardly a fizzled-out sparkler could be found.

As I persisted to the 1996 Olympics, I was sure this achievement would be everything I had always wanted. I had seen many hometowns celebrate their Olympians as town heroes. My family and friends, too, will be so happy and proud! All the doors to future opportunities would swing wide open, and paths would be obstacle-free. I would be considered an Olympian for the rest of my life. As the saying goes, "Once an Olympian, always an Olympian. Never former, never past."

Unfortunately, I did not attain Nirvana after the Games. When I made the Olympic field hockey team, I felt more relieved than happy. I recall being at the Olympics and feeling unhappy and alone because I received very little playing time. I distinctly remember saying to myself, "Andrea, you are at the Olympics. This is supposed to be a happy time, and you feel sorry for yourself." Achieving one of the most significant accomplishments of my life still did not fix what I was missing, which is why this book is so important to me: To help others with what I was missing.

We are told that pursuing and achieving accomplishments will sustain happiness, but I want to share how we can maintain an inner sense of joy, confidence, and self-mastery that brings us lasting success. Winning the inner Game brings more wins to the outer games we play. External accomplishments mean nothing without internal wins, and the pursuit of inner excellence and worthy goals makes the adventure the reward. The wrong game is thinking you will only feel good about yourself if you achieve whatever goal you are after. Those feelings of satisfaction are short-lived until the previous feelings of disappointment, self-loathing, and inner criticism return.

This book offers you and your team or system a path to self-mastery, which will enable you to be truly happy, satisfied, and at peace before, during, and after achieving your most important goals, and to accept your setbacks as temporary. Self-mastery is the way to winning more internally and externally.

## Grow in Self-Efficacy and Confidence

As you understand the pitfalls of only focusing on the game of outcomes, you will grow in self-efficacy. According to Albert Bandura, self-efficacy is "the belief in one's capabilities to organize and execute the courses of action required to manage prospective situations." Put more simply, it is a person's belief in their ability to succeed in a particular situation. Albert Bandura's theory outlines four sources of self-efficacy: (1) mastery experiences (experiencing success firsthand); (2) vicarious learning (success learned from seeing other people do it and gaining the confidence that you can do it too); (3) social or verbal persuasion (receiving encouragement, support, and coaching received from yourself or others); and (4) physiological states (feeling as if you can succeed).

### Confidence

Confidence, on the other hand, is the more generalized belief in one's ability to be more generally successful. Certainly, self-efficacy and confidence overlap and have similar qualities, such as belief in one's ability, positive impact on persistence and motivation, and stemming from positive experiences and encouragement. Self-efficacy tends to be task-specific, whereas confidence can be both broad and specific. The sources of self-efficacy are paths toward developing both confidence and self-efficacy. Here we will mainly focus on confidence, since that's what all athletes want and need to perform well.

The number one thing all performers want and need to consistently be at their best is confidence. The lack of it is the number one reason people come to see professionals like me. Performance confidence is believing in your ability to perform well in the upcoming competition, and confidence is key to achieving your highest levels of success. What do you notice when you see a confident performer? Do you see someone who believes in themselves and, hence, can perform to their optimal capacity? Have you noticed some people who are more relaxed than others when faced with pressure, and therefore can execute their plays as planned? Have you observed someone who has pride in their effort and performance, regardless of the result?

I have developed and taught countless athletes that confidence is a function of their preparation, belief, and past success:

**Confidence = (preparation + belief + past success)**

Recall a recent time when you were successful and reflect on what gave you confidence. Did you prepare yourself well by practicing and training with focus and purpose? Were you able to develop your skills so that you could trust your training and play with less conscious thinking and more trust in your ability to perform the skills without effort? Did you remember that you have been successful before and that you can dare to be successful again?

Another of Albert Bandura's four sources of self-efficacy is mastery experiences from past successes. Per my formula, if your belief is low, you can bolster your confidence with preparation. To bolster your present-moment confidence, you can recall past achievements and challenges you have overcome and times you have shown up for others in meaningful ways. If your number of past successes is low, you can elevate your confidence by increasing your preparation and belief in your ability to succeed as others have. If your preparation is low, you can bolster your beliefs and recall your past success. Increasing all three factors will help your confidence grow consistently.

Consistent confidence does not just come from being on a winning streak. When I was head of mental conditioning at IMG Academy, the father of a tennis player told me that he thought his son would be confident if he was winning and that it was my job to help his son win. I disagreed; my job was to help his son develop the mental skills of a confident performer so that he would be more likely to win because he trusted himself. I have worked with teenagers and adults who had convinced themselves of the misunderstanding that confidence comes from winning alone, and if you're not winning, then you have no reason to have confidence.

Confidence also doesn't come from others. Have you ever heard an athlete complain that they would be more confident if only others believed in them? Yes, Bandura's self-efficacy model tells us that verbal persuasion (encouragement from others) is a source of self-efficacy. However, if we are not getting that encouragement, other methods can bolster confidence. You are responsible for your confidence. As an athlete or performer, please understand that sustainable confidence is a skill under your control that only you can develop. Although social or verbal persuasion is one of the sources of self-efficacy, it may not be there when you need it, and you can't always rely on someone else to give you confidence. You can be your own source of verbal persuasion with how you talk to yourself. Like any skill, you can deliberately develop your confidence so it will be present and available when you call on it. There is no need to rely on someone giving it to you, particularly because that someone might not always be there!

One of my favorite quotes from Eleanor Roosevelt is, "No one can make you feel inferior without your consent." No one can take away your confidence unless you let them. That means you're 100 percent responsible for your trust in yourself. That doesn't mean you should lean toward arrogance or narcissism, which are unhealthy or false forms of confidence that arise from deep wounds and insecurity. Having healthy doubt is part of being a healthy performer, and can be a motivator or driver of action. I know for myself that having been afraid of performing below my abilities in physical fitness tests was highly motivating toward getting myself to the gym, on the track, and on the field for agility, sprints, plyometrics, weight-lifting, and skill development. The fear of looking bad was a definite motivator when I was training, and I still haven't determined whether this was a healthy fear.

Regardless, having that healthy doubt led to preparation, which is the most heavily weighted factor in confidence because it helps you gain mastery experiences. Physically and mentally rehearsing the same scenarios time after time and practicing countless reps are all part of preparation so you can be ready to respond when things go sideways. This is what the best of the best soldiers do. Special Ops and Delta Force, the most elite of the elite in specially trained forces, not only prepare for how they want to execute their plans but also for possible scenarios where things go wrong. They optimally train themselves to respond immediately when the most well-laid plans don't work. The Navy SEALs motto, from the Greek poet Archilochus, is, "We don't rise to the level of our expectations; we fall to the level of our training."

Most athletes prepare for how they want things to go instead of considering that things might not go that way. Instead of anticipating these surprises, unprepared athletes find themselves on their back heels, feeling overwhelmed and under-responsive, slow to react, delayed by surprise, and trying to solve these challenges on the fly. Your opponents will likely have something up their sleeves that you may not expect. Buck Brannaman, known as the Horse Whisperer, calls it "preparing for the unexpected." To increase your likelihood of responding quickly and accurately, practice your best responses and think through how you can prepare for those unexpected moments.

In baseball, for example, you don't leave your throwing, catching, and hitting up to chance and hope you'll have the skills when the moment calls for them. You practice these skills repeatedly throughout every practice session and in many scenarios, season after season and rep after rep, until they become so natural that you rarely have to think about how to do them. The game moves too fast for thinking to keep up, so the time for thinking about how to perform is during practice.

Do you hope that you will be confident on competition day? I have often suggested to top performers that "hope is not a strategy!" However, extensive research by Dr. Charles Snyder suggests that goals, agency, and pathways are the three sources of hope, which is a better strategy than crossing your fingers and hoping for the best! Hope can be developed and can be a part of your confidence strategy.

To build your confidence, follow these tips:

- have a process and stick to it
- don't measure yourself on results alone
- study others to emulate their processes, keeping in mind that success leaves clues (vicarious learning)
- remember what you did well (mastery experiences)
- develop consistent routines
- mentally rehearse giving your best performance—focus on what you can control
- identify and rely on your signature strengths

Conversely, eliminate or minimize these habits:

- putting yourself down when compared with someone else. Instead, learn what they do well and emulate their habits
- shaming yourself for your mistakes. Instead learn, correct, and move on from them

- pursuing perfectionism, which is the thief of joy
- having a nonstop Inner Critic. It's just an automatic habit of undisciplined thinking
- believing the negative thoughts you tell yourself (Don't believe everything you think!)
- letting someone else give you your sense of confidence or take it away
- thinking that your performance or your results make you a good or bad person
- taking other peoples' criticism to heart by feeling like less of a person
- engaging in negative self-talk, such as: "I'm so stupid. I suck. How could I have done that? I don't belong here"

Choose three strategies from the first list of habits that build confidence and put them into practice over the next four weeks, while working to eliminate three negative habits from the second list that erode your confidence.

### Consistent confidence and the myths of winning and competence

To find sustained success, you want to consistently show up with confidence. There are multiple instances of dynasty teams in which athletes who show up consistently and confidently dominate their opponents, win championships, and become exemplars of high performance. One of my favorite examples is the All Blacks, New Zealand's national rugby team, as discussed in James Kerr's book, *Legacy*.[2] Character, culture, teamwork, and humility are paramount to their success, and their Haka ritual is legendary. The Haka is the most effective pre-performance routine the world has ever seen.

The University of Connecticut's women's basketball team is also known for its dominance, which results from the compounding effects of consistent high-performance habits, routines, and team culture that preclude confidence. These habits focus on excellent fundamental execution and a team-first attitude. Research studies also support that consistent habits, routines, and an unwavering commitment to excellence are common traits and behaviors among Olympic champions.[3] Consistency and confidence are highly valuable qualities that any coach or teammate looks for when selecting athletes. Rather than showboating and self-promotion, dependability and consistency build trust between people, teams, and communities.

Team members should be able to count on each athlete or coach to consistently show up for every practice and competition being ready to compete fiercely. Other people know what to expect from someone who is reliable, consistent, and committed, whereas not knowing who will show up to perform at a practice or competition can be problematic. Consistency and confidence in habits, attitudes, and standards of excellence calms the system and frees up the performers to fully live up to their capabilities. The confident performer believes in their ability and competence to play their role well regardless of the circumstances and the pressures because they have consistently shown up and done the work. They have earned their confidence by consistently investing in themselves and their practice.

Consistency is not just doing the same repetitive and boring things day in and day out. In fact, coaches may throw in surprises and changes to help athletes develop responsiveness and adaptability to prepare them for unexpected situations that may occur during competition. Those who respond quickly and effectively tend to win. For example, Michael Phelps's coach, Bob Bowman, prepared Phelps to continue performing steadily even if he had an equipment malfunction. During the 200-meter Butterfly in the 2008 Olympics, Phelps's goggles filled with water, blinding him for the next 175 meters. Nevertheless, he not only won the gold but also broke a world record. Talk about confidence, preparedness, and reacting to surprises in a way that made him a champion on repeat!

## *Vicarious learning*

Vicarious learning is one of the four sources of Bandura's self-efficacy model, involving comparing someone else's competence to yours (Bandura, 1977). [4]You might notice yourself thinking, "If they can do it, I can do it." When I was boarding my two horses at a barn in Bradenton, Florida, these were the words I used when needing the confidence to race against the other boarders. I was head of mental conditioning at IMG Academy at the time, so I certainly knew a thing or two about confidence and doing things that scared me.

The barn was rustic yet functional, owned by a former racehorse trainer named John Barnhill. The manager, a 23-year-old spitfire named Kayla Guay, trained and exercised the prospect horses and was determined to gussy up the property. She is a hard worker with a generous spirit, and I looked forward to seeing her when I visited. We sometimes rode together, and I appreciated her old-soul personality and the knowledge she shared.

Soon, I found my heart growing fond of one of Barnhill's mares, named Shanhart, a six-year-old who never got to race. She had the heart for it but was removed from competition at a young age when a groomsman wrapped her legs too tight at the track, causing tendon problems. My heart won over my bank account, and the beautiful mare joined my pet family. Kayla had trained this very special chestnut mare whose name I changed to Zena the Warrior Princess, inspired by the TV superheroine Xena. I soon had two thoroughbreds, born to race, and one Friesian born to be pretty. Barnhill nicknamed Zen, my Friesian, "Pretty," and my thoroughbred Caesar as "Champ." Though I had owned horses for five years, I still felt like a beginner. I wanted to go fast, but the fear of getting injured held me back.

A local policeman named Joe, who also owned and boarded one of Barnhill's former racehorses, was racing his 17-hand beauty named Hope around the quarter-mile track at the barn. I arrogantly thought, "Wait a minute, I'm a better rider and athlete, so why am I scared of something he is doing regularly? If he can do it, then I can do it!" I challenged Kayla and Joe to a race in a sudden burst of boldness and confidence, and perhaps a bit of stupidity. I bought an old western saddle with a horn to hold on for dear life so that I could feel safer, and later that week I announced, "Okay, Joe and Kayla, today's the day. Let's race!"

We decided that the race would consist of three complete laps around the quarter-mile track and back to the start, with Joe riding Hope, Kayla riding my former racehorse Caesar, and me riding Zena. We agreed to trot to the starting line simultaneously and then take off. Hope and Caesar took off right at the starting line as their riders knew what they were doing, but Zena kept trotting. I egged her on as the galloping horses in front kicked dirt and sand into our faces. She started cantering and then exploded underneath me into her full gallop once she realized what was happening. We were far behind and mostly eating dirt. I had lost my stirrups but promised myself that I wouldn't fall off or give in to my fear! I held onto the saddle horn as if my life depended on it, feeling both exhilarated and a bit scared. The fear seemed to focus me in the moment. Zena felt so smooth and fast, and she began to gain on Hope and Caesar. She gave even more as we rounded the corner, and we won by a nose. What a thrill!

Experiencing the all-out speed of a racehorse, witnessing Zena's heart of gold, gaining the courage to overcome one of my fears, and winning the race were all made possible by gaining confidence through vicarious learning. I compared my competence to Joe's and said to myself that if he could do it, I could too. As you develop your competence, you might gain greater confidence when you compare yourself to someone else. You might be like Michael Jordan, arguably the GOAT of basketball and an all-around extraordinary athlete, who competed against his best self to stay motivated. No one else could really compete against him to make him better. The word "competition" means, "to seek together." Growth, learning, and fun happen when you get to test your skills against your previous best, as well as against others who are better than you, at least for now.

## Confidere: The Better to Best Versions of You

The Latin root of confidence is the word *confidere*, which means "with complete or intense trust" or "with fidelity." To trust means to confide in yourself or another person, such as a leader, or in a team, system, place, or process. The intent behind trust between two people is the spoken or unspoken agreement that each of them will do what they'd said they would do to the best of their ability. When trust is present, magic happens. Without trust, tension, conflict, unnecessary suffering, and lowered performance tend to occur. Trust is the secret sauce to any flourishing relationship or performance.

Trust implies that we expect to get the results or outcomes we are seeking, but in the rules of the Game of confidence ownership, the only guarantees are learning, growing, and aiming to perform better next time. Paradoxically, the intent of the Game is not to win more of the outcomes you desire but rather to win more trust, and many of those positive outcomes will result from this process. As I tell many of my clients, an important component of winning more trust is showing up as the better to best version of yourself as often as possible. The more consistent you are, the more others view you as dependable and trustworthy. Despite my daily intent to express my best self, I have yet to achieve a full day of 100 percent pure excellence. I string together moments of success like pearls on a necklace, but I often find that I could have responded more optimally or in a more refined way in many situations. My better to best versions of myself fit into a reasonable and consistent standard.

The improvement curve is asymptotic, meaning it never reaches a limit; it never arrives but rather continues onward toward infinity. Knowing that you will never reach a state of perfection means that not arriving there doesn't have to be a source of frustration. The imperfect, incomplete, and not-yet-best self is a source of inspiration to be appreciated, accepted, and celebrated, providing motivational momentum to keep going with a sense of eagerness to pursue greater improvement. Mastery and confidence are also asymptotic and are journeys of perfect imperfection where there is no final arrival. Mile markers are reached and celebrated, and challenges, setbacks, and disappointments appear and are managed, negotiated, and conquered. Learning should grow confidence rather than erode it.

When you're on a hike and have not yet reached the summit, you can focus on enjoying the unfolding of the hike, such as the beautiful scenery along the way toward reaching the best view at the top of the mountain. Wherever you are on the path is not less valuable just because you're not yet standing at the peak. If there's anything that I hope to emphasize here or that may jump out at you, it's to enjoy the process and the adventure, not just the destination. Reaching the summit is short-lived, and you don't stay on the summit of your hike for the rest of your life. On many occasions in my life, I was constantly gunning for and running toward the next achievement and forgot to enjoy the adventure along the way. We can all find happiness, success, and satisfaction at the intersection of progress, appreciation, and eagerness for more.

# Chapter 2

# What Are the Rules?

Rules and boundaries make any game more fun to play because they help you understand what to focus on, how to succeed, and in what ways you can creatively execute decisions with the presence of rules as guardrails. Abiding by the regulations of self-mastery will accelerate your consistent experience of achieving it. The word "decision" has the etymological root of "decir," which means "to cut off." When you decide on something, you cut off other options and commit to the process. Playing the Game of self-mastery or confidence ownership starts with a decision to play it well, including making the decision against focusing solely on results and the accumulation of external rewards and outcomes as your primary source of confidence and happiness.

Our overconsuming society tries to sell us on the idea that what will make us feel good is buying certain cars, clothes, shoes, and objects that make life more convenient, but these items tend to have a shelf life of only short-term pleasure. Accumulating external things also includes collecting awards, accolades, recognition, trophies, and large sums of money as sources of self-worth and confidence. External rewards and recognition can be enjoyable to receive as nice acknowledgments, but they will never sustain you as the source of your sense of confidence, ownership, and self-mastery.

The accumulation of stuff is a false measure of success and your value as a human. Without understanding self-mastery, which is putting your values into action, you will likely find yourself chasing unfulfilling conquests that result in short-lived satisfaction. Self-mastery is an inside-out game, not an outside-in one. Paradoxically, the more self-mastery you develop, the more likely you are to win external accolades as well as lead a life of sustained happiness and satisfaction.

## Rule #1: Create Goals

The Game impacts how you approach four primary domains in your life: Your self, your role (parent, athlete, coach, team around team member), your work or school, and your relationships. Each of these domains has identities you can select, which I call your Choice Identities. Playing the game involves focusing on getting to know who you are and who you want to be in these four primary domains of life.

Have you recently determined your most important goal in each of these four domains? You can choose which virtues, attributes, or values to rely on to achieve those goals and then decide on which specific, deliberate, and consistent behaviors are required to give yourself the best chance to reach them. Playing the Game involves focusing on implementing the processes and steps that are under your control. When you control your process, you can change course and adjust to improve your odds of success.

If you want to hit a target using a bow and arrow, you first learn how to hold the bow, load the arrow, aim, and release. Once you have released the arrow, you have no control over what happens except to accept your results and learn how to do it better next time. Thousands of arrows might be released before a shooter learns to consistently reach their target. When you aim at your targets, you become more confident in your process of learning from your results and adjusting to keep improving.

## Rule #2: Have Fun

One of the rules of how to play is to have fun, even while still taking yourself seriously enough to show up and do the work. If you're not having fun while learning, growing, and improving your skills and competencies, the Game becomes a grind instead of a source of joy. Playing the Game by beating yourself up, punishing yourself, and putting yourself down while practicing is against the rules. It's challenging to perform well when you are miserable inside. I spent years being extremely hard on myself, and although I achieved some decent success despite my self-loathing, I did not feel happiness or a sense of joy. Why suffer unnecessarily?

## Rule #3: Disconnect Self-Worth from Results

You need to accept that you're not your results. Remember when I made a goal to make the US field hockey team, but I still didn't feel accomplished? I'd thought my family would be so proud of me, and maybe they were, but I did not experience the celebratory enthusiasm I had expected and hoped for. Their response felt more like an acknowledgment that of course I achieved my goal because I had worked hard, and that's what I was supposed to do. The need I was most seeking to satisfy, getting approval from my family, was met with a dull, barely audible applause and a pat on the back that I hardly felt. Needless to say, it was a painful experience. My new belief became, "I guess that goal wasn't good enough ... I will have to keep proving that I'm worthy, acceptable, and lovable with higher levels of achievement."

I hadn't arrived after achieving the Olympics. I still didn't like myself and didn't enjoy life, and I mistakenly thought the next achievement would bring me the happiness, joy, approval, self-worth, and contentment I sought. No one had told me that chasing achievements for achievement's sake was like a dog chasing its tail.

My life pursuits now include enjoyment of the adventure, curiosity about what I'm learning about myself, and the process of clarifying my philosophy and growing as a person, not just meeting performance targets. Through the process of self-mastery, I no longer have an intense need for validation, approval, and pats on the back from others to feel a sense of self-worth. My new wins relate to my inner sense of self and my relationships, and the most satisfying part of my job is helping others win and progress in their self-mastery adventures.

Your worth is intrinsic to your being as a human. What your body, mind, and spirit are capable of is no less than a miracle of life. This is why my model starts with embracing your Human-First identity, as you are already valuable; you don't have to prove your worth. What you do with your inherently valuable self is where the fun, not the dread, should exist.

## Rule #4: Focus on the Process (80/20; 90/10)

Lanny Bassham, a two-time Olympic gold and silver medalist in shooting and author of the book *With Winning in Mind*, shares an incredible story about a golfer he worked with.[5] This professional golfer was not performing to his potential and was losing multiple rounds before he began working with Lanny on his mental game. The golfer started learning a highly disciplined approach of focusing 100 percent on hitting a good shot regardless of where his ball landed, his score, or in what precarious or optimal situation he found himself. Over a short period of time, he found himself at the 18th hole with a three-foot putt to finish his round at the end of a four-day tournament. He did not track his shots on each hole or know his overall score. He only cared about staying disciplined in his process, not focusing on his results or concerning himself with how his opponents were doing.

After reading the green, he locked in on his process, ran his routine, and made the shot. With his head still down and not knowing his standing, he heard the crowd erupting into cheers as he walked over to pick his ball out of the hole in his usual fashion. He noticed an unusual commotion around him, and when he lifted his head, he saw his wife running out toward him onto the green. He looked up at her and asked in disbelief, "Did I win?" Yes, he did!

Amazingly, this pro golfer had just sunk a "million-dollar" putt. Of course, all the other shots accumulated over four days, combined with his discipline to stick to his process, resulted in his victory. If he'd known where he was in the standing on the very last shot and had started to think about winning or losing, he might have succumbed to pressure and tightened up, as he had during previous tournaments. Instead, he trusted his process to hit his best shot regardless of the score, which ultimately led to his victory as a testament to the power of focusing on the adventure rather than on the destination. I love this story as a phenomenal example of the benefits of committing to playing each shot and focusing on each moment. Committing to the progress of learning, practicing to the best of your ability, and allowing the outcomes to take care of themselves often yields excellent results.

Lanny's teaching is to focus 100 percent on the process. I hold to the 80/20 principle that suggests you should keep 80 percent of your attention and efforts on the improvement process. This rule requires identifying what is 100 percent in your control, which includes your ACE (attitude, concentration, and effort). When working on your skills, drills, tactics, and strategies in your sport, focus 80 percent of your attention and evaluation on whether you are bringing your best attention, effort, and concentration to executing your skills at the speed of the sport, accurately, and under pressure.

Invest the remaining 20 percent of your attention and evaluation into whether you are heading in the right direction of your outcome goals. For example, when driving, you mindfully attend to the process of maintaining the speed limit, obeying traffic signs and lights, using a blinker, and paying attention to the road and the other drivers around you. However, you must also know how to reach your destination or trust a map that guides your directions. If you don't check in with where you are in relation to where you want to go, then the process of driving well will not necessarily get you to your desired outcome.

Did you connect passes to your teammates with accuracy and speed while under pressure on 80 percent of your attempts during your game? At more advanced levels, will your efforts be good enough to get you selected for the team you want to be on, earn you more playing time, and award you a starting position? Is your skill showing All-America prowess?

The higher their level in the sport, the more that athletes should focus on their process of executing accurately with speed while under pressure. Elite athletes' ratios shift to 90/10, where 90 percent of their efforts should focus on process, and 10 percent of their efforts should focus on evaluating their results. The paradox is that everyone expects outstanding results from high-level athletes, which prevents many of them from consistently performing. High performers understand that focusing on controlling their process to perform under tremendous pressure gives them the freedom and confidence to get the results they seek and others expect.

Begin practicing the 80/20 rule and notice how your confidence in your ability to execute starts to increase. The higher your performance levels, the more you should focus on your process in high-stakes environments. The positive results will come when you unleash your freedom to execute regardless of pressure, and the feelings of pressure about how to bring your A game will change from anxiety into excitement.

## Zone of control

The process of winning requires taking ownership of the controllables, meaning those tasks and actions that are 100 percent within the control of the individual performer. The more a person progresses in managing the controllables, the more they develop their system for winning. Making the mistake of focusing on things outside your control tends to result in misery, including in sports. Instead, focus your energy on learning, growing, and getting better. The results will come when you focus on the process. That's the only way to progress. Embrace the adventure of growth and improvement, and the results will naturally follow.

What is under your control? Your effort, concentration, attitude, work ethic, discipline, planning, time management, self-talk, body language, breathing, sleep schedule, diet, behavior, responses, appreciation, gratitude, curiosity, openness, and so on!

I have worked with many athletes who complained about their minutes of playing time, whether they were starting, what position they were playing, which player was asked to take the last shot of the game, and so on. The Confident Performer section of this book will further discuss listing the number of items within your control and those that aren't. In sports psychology, we call these variables the controllables and the uncontrollables. Focusing on what you can control tends to increase your confidence and focus your mind in the right direction to be able to perform in the way you are capable.

## Rule #5: Push Yourself

Go ahead and stand up if you're able and reach your hands as high as you can toward the ceiling. Really reach as high as you can go as if you want to touch the ceiling. Are you on the very tips of your tippy toes? Are you fully stretched up as if you are going to touch the ceiling? Once you are, hold your position and then reach up one more inch. Could you go a little more? Most people will eke out just a bit more at this point, and some a lot more. I call this the one-inch zone. This is the absolute best that you can give. When you are at your very peak, on your very edge, and it takes all of you to stay there, that's your very best. Remember what I first asked you to do? To reach as high as you can go. So, what happened? Why were you able to eke out even more?

Most people probably feel as if they were trying their best in a given situation, yet deep inside, we all know we may have had a little more to give. Sometimes we hold back because we're' not sure what will happen if we fully commit. We don't want to embarrass ourselves, be judged, or be deemed not "good enough"—especially if we have given our best. When you were up on your tippy toes, reaching as high as possible, I imagine it wasn't easy to hold yourself there. You can't always maintain your absolute best effort and stay in the one-inch zone, but we must train and push ourselves to be able to reach it. Indeed, I do not recommend that you always try to stay in the one-inch zone; the six fundamentals of a healthy performer include the necessity of having some downtime in the form of sleep, breathing, socioemotional connection, and communing with nature. But we must test ourselves to reach our highest point so we can know how to get there when we need it.

On the other hand, if you're always playing it safe and staying within your comfort zone of doing what you're already good at instead of stretching yourself to see what you can do, you will limit your growth. To grow, you must push yourself and risk failing to learn what you are capable of doing. The one-inch zone is the confident performer zone where you are willing to stretch your limits, do hard things, and make your new best your new baseline.

## Rule #6: Bring Your Better to Best Self

No one likes a cheater or a liar. In recent high-profile scandals, the World Anti-Doping Agency (WADA) banned certain Chinese swimmers and

Russian athletes from competition for having taken banned performance-enhancing drugs. Lance Armstrong, professional baseball players, and other athletes have cheated as well. Cheating and lying erode trust, which is the secret sauce and underlying magic of high performance. People cheat and lie as a form of immediate protection in response to the fears of retribution, rejection, shame, looking bad, disappointment, or punishment. Regardless of the impact on the person who lied or cheated, relationships around the person who lied or cheated begin to erode because relationships thrive on honesty, trust, and authenticity.

Making high performance and championship moments happen requires trusting yourself, your teammates, the leadership, and the game plan to bring out the best in yourself and others. Secrets, deception, and cover-ups that grow over time are often more hurtful than the original act of transgression. The downstream effects of cheating and lying are often more consequential than telling the truth or doing the right thing in the first place. Self-mastery and confidence ownership require doing the right thing when no one is watching. Feelings of confidence and trust only manifest when honesty and integrity are at the forefront of a relationship. Leaders who admit to their mistakes, accept responsibility, and are honest about their actions contribute to building trust, whereas denial, dismissing, blaming, or shifting responsibility erodes trust. With a willingness to admit wrongdoings and mistakes and do better when we know better, we grow into self-mastery and authentic confidence.

# Chapter 3

# Who Are the Players?

Parents, Athletes, Coaches, and TAT members make up the players or roles in this winning system. An athlete's closest and most important relationships can be with coaches, parents, teammates, and members of their performance and health support team. TAT members are typically athletic trainers, strength and conditioning coaches, nutritionists or sports dietitians, data scientists, academic advisors, and sports psychologists or mental performance coaches. Bonds form when a group experiences a gauntlet of emotions concurrently, performs hard work together, and pursues a meaningful goal. Cohesion and trust grow from pursuing excellence and learning to surf the emotions of wins, losses, and tribulations.

An athlete learns to recognize that they cannot successfully grow and win without these important people playing a role in their development. And all the players form a positive team culture. Parents learn from each other and form friendships and meaningful bonds with other parents as they watch their children develop. TAT members collaborate and learn from one another, the coaches, and the athletes, and get to work together and bring their best selves to contribute to doing meaningful work toward the betterment and growth of the athletes. For the entire system of parents, athletes, coaches, and TAT, leaving ego at the door helps optimize the system and each role in it. Everyone can walk away as better humans and performers because of having one another's backs.

## The Players, the PACT

All four roles within the PACT are important parts of a winning system. Whereas most athletic systems focus solely on the athletes themselves, it is important to optimize each of the roles (parents, athletes, coaches, and TAT) because they are all vital to producing extraordinary outcomes. Programs should start with being athlete-centric, but the best ones must focus on developing the whole system. In particular, the system, or team, cannot ignore parents because they play exceptional roles. Most performance psychology practitioners focus primarily on the athletes and may occasionally include the coaches, and coaches and administrators often treat involving parents as an afterthought, viewing them as a group to tolerate instead of leverage. Many coaches even want to push out parents and keep them away from the team, thinking that parents should only write checks, drop off the athletes on time, and accept whatever the program is doing without complaint so as to leave the coaching to the professionals.

We've all heard stories about out-of-control parents who argue with referees, taunt opponents, and even go to disturbing levels of antagonizing their own coaches, children, or their children's teammates. Most sporting organizations have rules for fans, parents, and spectators because their troublesome behavior can be a source of unnecessary stress for the players and coaching staff, and other parents, friends, and spectators who are just trying to cheer on their team and enjoy the game.

The negative assumption that parents are a nightmare became so prominent in athletic departments that I changed my thinking from how to leverage the power of parents instead of ignore it. I recognized that the traditional pre-season one-hour talk that's typically offered to parents of athletes was not enough to change their behavior and empower them to play positive roles in the system of winning. My recommendation is for people in all parts of the system, including parents, coaches, athletes, and the TAT members, to use the same mental training system. All roles should agree to play the Game of self-mastery and confidence ownership to serve something bigger and speak the same language to reinforce the commitments and goals of the whole team. The results are exponential, not additive. (See the Winning Systems Psychology program in Appendix B.)

## Parents

Parents or guardians are the first adults, teachers, and role models children depend on to care for them. They are life-giving and life-serving for vulnerable, young, developing beings, and it is important for parents or guardians to do their best to be present and emotionally available in healthy ways for their child's development and growth.

## Coaches

Coaches also are incredibly important role models in an athlete's life. Most athletes work hard to please their coach and parents by performing well. Although athletes prefer praise over criticism most days of the week, the child-athlete still should want to be corrected or taught a better way. Children thrive with boundaries. Knowing their limits helps them develop a sense of safety and security and makes the world feel less overwhelming. Rules in a sport make the game more fun, fair, and safe to play, and having structure, discipline, and affection helps humans thrive.

## TAT

TAT members play meaningful roles in an athlete's life. Strength and conditioning (S&C) coaches can be strong forces of nature as they push athletes to greater physical prowess in strength, speed, agility, power, balance, mobility, flexibility, and endurance. Physical improvements can elevate an athlete's belief and confidence in themselves. The TAT is vital to a sports team's success as the intensity, stakes, and pressure to perform increase. I have been on the receiving end of effective TATs at the University of Iowa and on the US National field hockey team. I have also been on the giving and directing end of being a member of a TAT and as a director overseeing all the TATs at UPenn and the mental conditioning coaches at IMG Academy in Bradenton, Florida.

TAT members work closely together so the correct information is delivered to the athlete by the right person, ensuring that the athlete hears the message. It would make no sense to have information delivered to an athlete by a subject-matter expert with whom the athlete did not have trust or a relationship. This level of collaboration between TAT members is critical to athletes' development and keeping everyone on the same page. It requires that TAT members leave their egos at the door and focus on what's best for the athlete and the team.

In that vein, successful S&C coaches need to know how much to push, when to back off, and when to help each athlete make a wise decision to take time to rest for a full recovery. As an example, take Cory Waltz, whom I hired at UPenn as the Director of Strength and Conditioning for our athletic department. He developed a system of autonomy whereby athletes could communicate with their S&C coach about their fatigue, soreness, and readiness to perform. Each athlete chose whether they were in a green, yellow, red, or black zone to train that day, and S&C coaches would adjust the athlete's training regimen depending on their selected zone. Green means "go—let's push;" yellow means "slow down, perhaps don't move up in weights or don't go to failure;" red means "light stretching, walking, or recovery activities such as rolling or using a Theragun;" and black means "get out of the gym to take care of yourself with a nap." If the athlete consistently selected a low-energy zone, a conversation ensued to find out what was happening.

Tired, sore, and unmotivated athletes who are on the brink of injury from overtraining serve no one. The S&C coach often has an eye for seeing an athlete's potential and can get much more out of them than even what the athlete thought was possible. Many cognitive and/or emotional loads can affect an athlete outside the sports arena, such as various academic, family, and personal stressors, which can affect the athlete's physical load. A rested, ready-to-go, strong, powerful, fast, agile athlete tends to be far more confident in their physical capabilities than an athlete who is out of shape, tires quickly, and hence cannot move as well or think clearly. Vince Lombardi repeated General Patton's quote by reminding his players that, "Fatigue makes cowards of us all." Indeed, a great S&C coach can contribute highly to an athlete's confidence, overall fitness, and well-being.

A certified athletic trainer (ATC) or physiotherapist can also play a decisive mentoring role in an athlete's life, especially if the athlete is injured, on a return-to-sport plan, or aiming to prevent a potential re-injury. The ATC may provide emotional support and understanding as well as structure and discipline to the athlete so they can follow their healing protocol and rehabilitation process, as well as intuiting when to push the athlete in the rehabilitation process and when to help them manage expectations. An athlete's confidence in their rehabilitation program plays a key role in whether they will feel ready to return to their sport. When a trainer and athlete execute a systematic, progressive program, an athlete can feel eager and excited to get back out there, but a poorly executed or mediocre rehabilitation experience tends to leave athletes feeling fearful about returning too soon and risking getting re-injured. A trusting relationship instills confidence in an athlete while they embark on a challenging road to regaining full readiness to compete again.

## Other TAT Team Members

### *Sports nutritionist or dietician*

The sports nutritionist or dietitian plays an essential role for the athlete, especially when they are working closely on a particular weight gain or loss goal or a lean muscle mass improvement plan, or on issues of body image, disordered eating concerns, or relative energy deficiency in sport (RED-S) syndrome, or preparing for or recovering from surgery. Maintaining privacy and confidentiality between the athlete and dietitian is vital for building a trusting relationship. As an athlete experiences performance and health improvements, such as an increase in lean muscle mass due to their diet, they feel greater control over themselves and their choices. The athlete's confidence, sense of self-worth, and empowerment positively contribute to their sense of self-mastery.

### *Sports psychologist or mental performance coach*

Sports psychologists or mental performance coaches play critical roles in enhancing an athlete's positive sense of self, confidence, and mental health. For instance, they can help athletes advocate for themselves with coaches and teammates by teaching athletes effective communication skills or helping them understand and express their needs and concerns. Sports psychologists or mental performance coaches can also help athletes gain perspective and insight to better solve or approach a problem in their sport or in their life and provide emotional space to say things out loud so their inner dialogue can shift beneficially. Sports psychologists also help coaches with their mental performance and can teach them how to communicate differently to better meet the diverse needs of athletes.

Notably, mental performance coaches help define and develop team culture to increase the chances of team success while optimizing individual athlete contributions. Some head coaches believe they're responsible for their athletes' mental performance and team culture as well as the strength and conditioning of their athletes. As sports performance research advances and overall competition increases, the coaches and administrators who collaborate with experts in the physical, mental, and emotional lives of athletes, coaches, and parents have a greater chance of their teams winning and having positive sporting experiences.

## Data scientist

Data scientists collect and analyze various physical, mental, and emotional health data to identify patterns of key performance indicators. Wearable devices have made sports measurements incredibly robust, but it can be confusing as to which ones to select and what data to focus on. Hundreds of companies offer an array of sports performance measurement devices, which include smartwatches, fitness trackers, heart rate monitors, GPS trackers, motion sensors, accelerometers, biometric devices, force plates, biomechanical or gait analysis systems, motion capture systems, and VO2 and lactate analyzers. As more sports performance technology products and services enter the marketplace, the need for data scientists will increase. Sorting valid and reliable technology from what's fraudulent, oversold, or preposterous can save athletes, teams, and programs time, money, and effort, and can reduce or mitigate injury.

Athletes have different needs and require fair but not equal treatment because fairness is not sameness. Thus, data science objectively optimizes each athlete's needs and discourages playing favorites or treating some athletes poorly due to personal biases or judgments. The collection of data on key performance health metrics empowers coaches, athletes, and TAT members to make better decisions on individualizing practices, training, and recovery. Key performance indicators might include sleep quality and quantity, fatigue and soreness, perceived exertion, emotional load, cognitive load, volume of work, training load over time, heart rate variability, speed, acceleration or deceleration, force plate analysis, jump metrics, acute to chronic workload ratio, hydration status, and the like. With an exorbitant number of possible data points, and the need to figure out the key metrics for the particular athlete relative to their position, age, goals, years in training, state of injury or compromise, the time of the season, and a host of other factors make the role of the data scientist critical to the health, safety, and performance of each athlete and to the success of the overall team.

Using data visualization tools to present findings clearly and compellingly is a key aspect of data utilization. It helps coaches, athletes, and TAT members make optimal decisions that enhance their understanding and preparedness. Data utilization aims to mitigate injury risk and increase the safety and performance of each athlete. Data do not make the decisions; they inform decisions. I prefer calling the decisions used to make optimal athlete-management decisions data-supported, not data-driven. Coaches, practitioners, and athletes can have better conversations by asking better questions, having curiosity, and being more open regarding trends, decisions, and strategies that support each athlete's whole health and performance.

## Director of sports performance

When I was the director of sports performance at UPenn, I oversaw a team of 20 full-time providers and 18 interns or practicum-level graduate students who cared for the almost 1,000 student-athletes in the Penn athletics department. I called our TAT members the gel of each sports team, as we were the providers that bound the academic, athletic, and social lives of the student-athletes by caring about the whole human and healthy performer.

In my decades of experience, I've noticed that athletes may have closer relationships with some TAT members than with others. Also, some TAT members may work more closely with certain athletes because of the needs of each individual athlete. These bonds between TAT members and athletes are the lifeblood of safety, belonging, and care that an athlete feels on a team, especially if the athlete is not feeling "seen" by a coach.

As the director of sports performance, I cared less about the expertise of the person on the TAT who delivered the information to the athlete and more about the trusting relationship and rapport the athlete had with certain members. The culture we created at UPenn focused on helping one another shine so the student-athletes could have the best possible experiences.

## Collaborators, Competitors, Coopetition, and Comcourage

The best team members work with each other as collaborators, not against one another. I call it *coopetition*, a term that combines cooperation and competition. When you cooperate and compete simultaneously, you will bring out the best in yourself and others. This concept is crucial for team dynamics, as it fosters a culture where athletes can challenge each other to reach greater heights. Team members can be competitive in generating the best ideas and approaches to help the team win while caring for systems, learning, and optimization. Parents, athletes, coaches, and TAT members must also be on the same page, talking the same language of self-mastery and how to play it well. When parts of a system work against each other, unnecessary friction erupts and pulls energy away from the more critical tasks. Making efforts to win and execute should be the focus, instead of blaming, shaming, complaining, denying, or dismissing. By cooperating with our teammates and opponents, together we can seek the highest versions of our skills and selves in competition.

Competition is thrilling when a performer approaches it with curiosity and openness. It's about discovering that you can give it your all, and trust that you can go deeper if needed. The joy of competition lies in the unfolding of wills, skills, training, tactics, strategy, and execution between competitors. No one knows the score or who will win—that's the beauty of it. Just because you lost before does not mean you will lose today, and just because you have won in the past does not mean today's results are guaranteed. We play to grow, learn, and hopefully have fun while playing the game and competing. The goal is to express our full potential, giving it our all with the aim of winning.

When we bring our best practices and training efforts to the game, our teammates also get to grow. When all team members collaborate by cooperatively competing, the team gets better. Your teammates can make you better, and you can do the same for them. Fun, playful banter, and growth all occur at the juncture of competing, cooperating, and collaborating, making all the hard work worthwhile. Get after it and work on improving each other, thereby giving your team the best chance to win.

# Chapter 4

# What Are the Roles and Responsibilities?

## Parent (STEP)

As the starting point for most children getting into sports, parents tend to be one of the biggest influences on an athlete in providing role modeling, encouragement or discouragement, creating the home ecosystem, giving advice, setting boundaries, saying no or yes, and providing opportunities through financial support. And, of course, parents had to come first to create the mnemonic acronym PACT!

To parent is to "bring forth" or produce, bringing to mind growth, development, encouragement, and summoning what is already present. Just like bringing forth and encouraging a baby's first steps, parents can remember that they help their child STEP (see, teach, act as an exemplar, remain present) into their next phases of growth and development. Of course, parental responsibilities go well beyond the STEP acronym, but it's a helpful reminder for parents about their roles in the winning systems model.

### S = SEE (Supporter, Encourager, and Embracer of Challenges)

The S in STEP stands for another acronym, SEE, which itself stands for supporter, encourager, and embracer of challenges. The SEE step requires learning who your child is. Comedian Tig Notaro said it best when she said, "It's not the child's responsibility to teach their parents who they are, it's the parents' responsibility to learn who their child is." Parents observe the areas in which their child needs support and encouragement or when they need to face a challenge to develop emotional and mental skills such as the resilience to do hard things. The parent will not always be correct in knowing exactly when to support, encourage, or embrace challenges, as there are no definite correct answers on how to parent. Embracing challenges can be as simple as allowing your child to try a new sport or activity and praising their efforts, even if they might not succeed at first. These actions help build resilience and confidence in your child. The more that a parent can ask effective questions of their child, the greater the opportunity becomes for the child to increase their self-awareness so they can stop to reflect on how they can take more ownership and accountability over how they show up, instead of blaming others for their circumstances.

Some situations call for all three actions concurrently. Children need to be supported and encouraged to figure out challenges independently and face the consequences of their actions without the parents doing the task for them or plowing them a path to make it easy. Confidence, self-esteem, and resilience develop when a child faces and embraces challenges, finds solutions, gains feedback, and further develops their skills, regardless of the results. To quote Michael Jordan, six-time NBA champion, "I've failed over and over again in my life, and that's why I succeed." Likewise, children need to face challenges over and over again to succeed, but should not feel like they are drowning in being overwhelmed.

When parents plow the path or remove any obstacles or challenges in their child's path to ensure that the child quickly reaches a goal, they are often called "bulldozer parents" and "snowplow parents." These parents may intervene in school or sports situations to ensure their child's success, often at the expense of the child's independence and resilience. A snowplow parent is similar, but they go even further, actively seeking out and removing potential obstacles before their child even encounters them. The detrimental effect of these parenting styles is that a child doesn't learn to navigate setbacks or face adversity and hardship, hence the parent's well-meaning intentions can result in highly negative consequences for their child. Children of bulldozer parents have increased risks of psychological fragility and becoming avoidant or anxious in the face of challenges.

Children of bulldozer parents, as compared with children of parents who don't exhibit these traits, tend to have poorer emotional regulation and coping skills and struggle with more anxiety, depression, indecision, and other mental health-related issues. They tend to have less self-efficacy and more self-doubt, which shows up academically and athletically. These children are more likely to develop a greater sense of entitlement and demand that others do as they wish and may expect others to remove obstacles for them. They're less likely to notice others' needs as they are often self-focused on getting their own needs met.

In bulldozer parents' overinvolved efforts to protect and be of service to their children, healthy growth is hindered. Paradoxically, the parents become the very barriers to their children's success that they intend to remove! Parents' efforts to balance their involvement with respecting a child's independence are crucial. This balance not only contributes to the joy and satisfaction of their children's sporting experiences but also reassures parents that they are on the right track. When parents rescue a child, not from physical, mental, or emotional danger as would be appropriate, but from facing hardships, disappointments, losses, and setbacks, and by "fighting" the battles for their child, a child's emotional growth and mental health stagnate.

I have noticed far more parental involvement in the present generation of children, teenagers, and college-age students than there was in my generation. My parents expected me to speak directly with coaches and teachers at a young age if I had questions or concerns about my grades, athletic performance, playing time, or position. When a child can grow and learn, a parent can SEE (be a supporter, encourager, and embracer of challenges) and do what's best for the child's ability to manage their way through challenges with positive growth. Achieving this balance is a secure and confident approach that parents can adopt.

## T = Teacher/Disciplinarian

To discipline means to teach, not to punish. Parents are a child's first teachers. In the teaching role, a parent practices asking effective questions from an open and curious place to help engage their child. Listening carefully to the child's answers without needing to answer their question for them allows the parent to pick up on subtle cues about preferences, interests, biases, or unspoken anxieties and fears. Showing interest and responsiveness even when the parent disagrees helps a child feel heard. Patience, empathy, and a calm demeanor go a long way when connecting with a young person. Tailoring your message so the student can hear the lesson in it facilitates the successful reception of the message. A child who is actively listening ensures that learning can take place.

The disciplinarian can be a more complex role for some parents, particularly when they aim to be the child's friend instead of their parent. One of the key roles of a parent is to set boundaries and expectations regarding which behaviors are okay and not okay. Enforced rules, limits, and expectations foster respect, responsibility, and discipline primarily for positive learning. Depending on the child's age, involving them in the decision-making can foster ownership, but the parent should have the final say in the household.

## E = Exemplar

An exemplar is defined as a role model or pattern to be copied or imitated. We know that children watch their parents, mimicking sounds, facial expressions, mannerisms, gestures, tones of voice, expressions, inflections, and the like at a very early age. Learning grows into self-discovery. Children experience cognitive dissonance when a parent tells them one thing to do or not do and then does the opposite thing themselves. Cognitive dissonance, or mental discomfort, occurs when there is inconsistency between internal cognition (beliefs, knowledge, attitudes) and external actions or behaviors. When there is incongruence between what a parent says and does, a child will feel hesitant or doubtful about the correct actions.

By being an exemplar for your child, you're modeling the beliefs, expectations, and desires that you have for them with words and actions. Admitting when you have made a mistake and modeling vulnerability takes courage. Admitting when you're wrong and repairing a relationship are essential ways of exemplifying character, virtues, and values. Being an exemplar plays a critical role in helping your child grow and contribute to the systems in which they operate. When you're right with yourself, you contribute positively to those around you. Teams fare better when parents are part of the system, modeling self-mastery behaviors and attitudes to impressionable minds.

A child is far more likely to believe what a parent does over what they say. As Ralph Waldo Emerson said, "What you do speaks so loudly that I cannot hear what you say." Children pick up values, beliefs, and behaviors by intentionally or unintentionally observing and mimicking their parents and other adults. Children also pick up their parents' subtle and not-so-subtle fears, stresses, and anxieties. Conversely, children pick up their parents' self-assuredness about handling situations maturely, ethically, and empathically for the benefit and balance of all involved.

Research studies demonstrate that parents' constructive feedback, emotional availability, and nurturing guidance influence a teenager's self-esteem and emotional intelligence.[6] Authoritative parenting (versus authoritarian, permissive, or uninvolved styles of parenting) encourages independence and is supportive and non-punitive. It sets clear boundaries and enforces consequences, resulting in children who develop more of an internal locus of control and greater social connectedness, interdependence, and healthier self-esteem as compared with children raised in the other three less effective parenting styles.

## P = (Giver of) Presence

Giving attention and presence to any human is an investment of focus and energy that demonstrates a level of care. When complemented with respect, warmth, curiosity, interest, and openness, giving one's presence is the ultimate act of support. Being distracted by your anxieties sends a message that your child or other loved ones are less important, so finding outlets for managing your stress and stabilizing your emotional regulation are key to giving your presence to others. The six fundamentals of a whole-person and healthy performer are critical for overscheduled parents who are juggling the many roles they play.

A great resource for parents is Brian Johnson's book, *Areté: Activate Your Heroic Potential*, which I highly recommend.[7] In a chapter called "Three Parenting Tips," Johnson discusses the importance of being an exemplar, having a mindful presence, and helping your children embrace challenges. Influenced by Carol Dweck's book, *Growth Mindset*, Johnson inspires parents across the planet to show up for their children in heroic ways.[8]

Olympic shooting champion Lanny Bassham also wrote a helpful book called, *Parenting Champions*. He states that the most important question for parents to ask themselves is, "What is most important to you, what did your children accomplish, or who they become?"[9] I've observed that parental pressure seems to be increasing for kids at increasingly younger ages to win, be in the starting lineup, get more minutes of playing time, and make the all-star and travel teams. The goals of encouraging personal growth, learning, and character development in children may therefore become lost. Who a child becomes should matter more than what they accomplish, as the nature of their character will be present in everything they do in life. The pursuits of college scholarships, seeking name recognition in collegiate sports, and entering professional sports careers have parents and coaches pushing early sport specialization such that kids at increasingly younger ages end up playing year-round just to keep up with everyone else. The pressures of early specialization contribute to early burnout, overuse injuries, increased anxiety, and a lack of joy. Parents also experience pressures from sports clubs for their children to travel to competitions outside the state.

I do not encourage early specialization nor competitive year-round training in a single sport for any athlete under the age of 14, and even age 14 may be too young. The professionalization of youth sports has turned recreation and leisure into an incentivized approach for early talent identification. Those who emphasize specialization argue that it will increase athletes' chances of winning scholarships and sponsorships and achieving Olympic and professional success. Indeed, the NCAA's ruling on name, image, and likeness (NIL) campaigns has already changed the face of collegiate sports as multiple athletes are winning six-figure or more deals with sponsors, and universities or boosters pay athletes to attend their schools above the full-ride scholarship. However, research studies have shown that athletes who make it to the pros or to the Olympics and have the greatest longevity in their sport, actually played two or more different sports when they were growing up.[10]

A father recently shared with me that his six-year-old daughter's gymnastic club leaders pressured the family to fly from Salt Lake City, Utah, to San Antonio, Texas, for an invitational meet just so that his daughter could be with the team, walk across the beam, and do a penny drop from the uneven bars. The family spent close to $3,000 for a weekend trip and what he deemed to have been a "ridiculous expectation" of the club. He and his wife could have turned it down of course, but their daughter was afraid of missing out since most of the other girls were going.

## Athlete (LEO + F)

To characterize the athlete's role, I use the acronym LEO, which stands for learner, efforter, and optimizer. The word "leo" in the context of a lion also symbolizes courage, nobility, ferocity, strength, power, and natural leadership. Lions are part of a pride that relies on one another, being the only cats that live in a group, and are known for their loyalty. A lion's personality is typically decisive, confident, and communicative. They're self-sufficient and goal-oriented, as well as team players. These are all great descriptions of a successful athlete. Notice that the "p-word"—perfectionist—is not one of the roles of the athlete, and I think it should be removed from the vocabularies of athletes, coaches, and parents. In athletics, there is excellent, outstanding, astounding, breathtaking, awe-inspiring, stupefying, wondrous, and spectacular, but not perfect. Perfectionism tends to get in the way of performance.

### L = Learner

The primary role of an athlete is to be an active, open, and curious learner. Athletes are responsible for learning all they can about the skills, tactics, and strategies of their sport and as much as they can about taking care of the body and mind so they can do what they are asking their body to do and what the competitive environment demands from them. All athletes must first learn general foundational movement skills such as running, jumping, balancing, throwing, kicking, catching, and coordinating before they can learn and refine their sport's specific skills, tactics, and strategies. The learner mentality, also called growth mindset, is a primary responsibility of the athlete in a winning system. An athlete's responsibility is to be a student of the game.

## E = Efforter

Athletes invest far more time, effort, and energy into practice than in competition. Putting the right amount of effort into practice and training to learn the necessary skills and eventually execute them with the speed and accuracy of competition takes countless hours of deliberate practice. Being an efforter does not necessarily mean overexertion that gets in the way of execution, like when a golfer grips too tightly and creates unnecessary tension in their swing. An efforter, as defined here, is a diligent, focused worker. No one who wants to succeed can get away with minimum, lackluster work. Those who have been relying on their talent alone as everything comes easily and who have little to no work ethic are eventually surpassed by those with less natural talent but a great work ethic. As Tim Notke, a high school basketball coach, said, "Hard work beats talent when talent doesn't work hard."

As athletes learn their sport's skills, tactics, and strategies, they must put in significant effort to understand what their body can execute, adapt sports skills to their body, and decide how to apply the right skills to the right situation. This effort is not just a requirement, but a crucial part of their skill development, making their hard work even more significant. The best and most inspiring athletes are those who are humble enough to know they need to practice and are confident enough to take smart, calculated risks during their practice sessions to stretch their limits. GOATs like Kobe Bryant, Shaun White, and Simone Biles are all known for their exceptional work ethics. They put the extra time into their training to ensure they could respond with extraordinary precision when the pressure was on.

Someone who aims to improve in each practice session and consistently applies what they learned will eventually progress, if not leapfrog, past their competition. If a naturally gifted athlete reaches the top, they will not stay there long without hard work. Show me a consistent winner, and I'll show you a hard worker. Hard workers find ways to persevere through adversity, frustration, and mistakes. They figure out what works for them and become more innovative and strategic to compensate for not necessarily being the fastest, strongest, or most athletic initially. Of course, athleticism must be present to reach the top of your sport, but pairing talent with work ethic makes you a force. If you add humility, confidence, and a willingness to learn and grow constantly, you have a recipe for becoming one of the greats.

## O = Optimizer

The optimizer is driven by finding ways to get better over time. Optimizers need to be creative in how they optimize every part of their game, as they know they might need to respond quickly to challenges from an opponent that they've never competed against.

Optimizers recognize that learning and growth are asymptotic, meaning there is never a finish line to arrive at. For athletes who optimize every dimension of themselves as healthy humans and confident performers by committing to self-mastery, their process and progress will undoubtedly develop and allow them to surpass their genetically gifted potential.

## + F = FUN

The "f-word" sometimes means "failure" or "fear," which athletes often experience in a combination of ways that include fear of failure, fear of disappointing oneself or others, and fear of looking bad. In this acronym, however, the "+" in + F refers to being positive, and in this context, the "f-word" is "fun." Fun does not mean being silly and not taking your performance seriously enough to show up and give your best. It does mean that focus follows fun because it's fun to give your best while executing your skills at the current level you are capable of.

Emphasizing the fun in performance is what brings feelings of joy and satisfaction to an athlete's achievements. Enjoying the camaraderie of your teammates and executing the plays you have worked on in practice and training is fun; sports are fun; being with your teammates is fun; and being skillful is fun. If you bring your positivity and sense of fun to the competition arena, the likelihood of performing well will increase.

It's challenging to perform well when you are miserable. Rarely does high performance come from feeling down or being destructive. Some people can muster achieving high performance in a low state, but few can sustain their performance when negativity dominates their mental state. Fun brings out your creativity and sustains your engagement and willingness to keep going even in the face of adversity. Make it fun, and you will likely increase your consistency, confidence, longevity, and high performance.

## Coach (SEED)

The coach's role is to plant SEEDs (be a supporter, exemplar, educator, and decision-maker) and tend the garden of helping their athletes grow. Just as each plant has a unique expression and has different needs regarding soil, sun, water, or pH balance, each athlete is unique and has individualized needs that require coaches to be empowered to tailor their methods in order to meet them. Some athletes like a more direct and demanding approach and respond well to more heat, whereas others need a more encouraging approach with less direct sunlight. All athletes should be treated with dignity, respect, and fairness, but they should not be treated the same because each athlete is a unique individual. Fairness means that coaches shouldn't play favorites. The athletes know it and resent it when coaches play favorites. Treat each athlete with care and respect and you are apt to get the most from them.

## S = Supporters

As a supporter, your role is to motivate and bring out the best in your athletes for the greater good. This involves acknowledging their efforts for a job well done but without over-celebrating. You're also there to support the athletes' tears, disappointments, and sorrows. Your positive presence, undivided attention, and empathetic listening without trying to fix or gloss over the pain can provide comfort and motivation for your athletes to persist in the face of adversity.

Supporters point out precisely what the person did well, giving them the courage to face the areas they need to improve in. Supporters are not Pollyannish; they do not make everything out to be sunshine and rainbows, but rather they tell the truth in a way that others can hear it and make the change. There is no blaming, shaming, or complaining. Communication should be clear, direct, and concise, getting to the point without harping, dwelling, or slighting the truth and tailoring the message to the individual so they can truly hear it.

## E = Exemplars

Coaches must exemplify the virtues and values of what they believe in and expect from their athletes. Like parents, coaches who practice what they preach are more successful at connecting with their athletes while building and maintaining trust. Depending on their age and experience, coaches may or may not be able to perform the skills of the sport to the highest level. However, coaches who were once athletes of the sport and can credibly demonstrate the skills they want the players to implement may deepen players' trust, respect, and admiration. However, demonstrating skills is not required if the coach knows the sport well enough to instruct the athletes and take them to a higher level, and meeting the athletes where they currently are and helping them grow.

Trust is built through caring for, respecting, and understanding your athletes. Just as you want your athletes to listen to you, you should also listen to them to be better aligned with your feedback, goals, and expectations. When you model honesty, transparency, clarity, and open communication, your athletes are more likely to reciprocate. Topics such as playing time, positions, team dynamics, attitudes, focus, and execution all require this level of honesty and transparency. Otherwise, secretive behaviors can lead to mistrust and distortions of the facts. Coaches who admit to making mistakes when they don't know something or don't have enough information and are willing to repair relationships when they have been unfair or wrong, exemplify important skills for their athletes and contribute to building trust in the system. Recall that trust is the secret sauce and the magic behind winning teams.

## E = Educators

Coaches are educators who teach, guide, monitor, give feedback, encourage, and correct the attitudes, behaviors, and performance execution of athletes. They build trust, cohesion, positive competition, and culture. Coaches develop athletes' skills, tactics, roles, and understanding of strategies. They teach teamwork and develop each individual's abilities to enhance overall team success. Coaches impart their knowledge and experience in the sport by explaining, asking effective questions, demonstrating techniques, reviewing film, letting other members of the staff teach, letting athletes help each other, drawing out plays, reinforcing what works, correcting what needs to be adjusted, and fostering relationships between themselves and each athlete. The most successful coaches build an environment where each athlete feels individually valued, challenged, supported, and validated, and that their contributions uniquely strengthen the team.

I encourage all coaches to eliminate scolding, yelling, and confrontational communication. When you yell, you're not fulfilling your role as an educator or allowing key sports lessons to translate into valuable life skills. Communicating loudly across the field is different, but it should be rare. Although yelling often stems from how coaches were treated as athletes or what they've seen, it reflects a lack of control. In response to being yelled at, athletes who already have heightened anxiety may involuntarily have their frontal cortex (the decision-making area of the brain) shut down due to the fear of making more mistakes. When athletes physically tighten up due to stress, their coordination decreases, and their self-doubt increases when they cannot move with freedom. A coach who constantly yells may promote a culture of fear, which could have short-term gains but usually results in long-term negative consequences on the mental health and motivation of athletes, which also negatively impacts the athletes' sense of dignity.

When a coach teaches the hows and whys of the sport and asks probing questions, athletes can problem-solve in real time, gain greater self-awareness and insights, test solutions, make decisions without fear of punishment, and take more ownership in their self-development. The athletes can more quickly gain self-mastery and mastery of the sport. These athletes tend to be more motivated and committed to their growth for the benefit of themselves and the team, which is the ultimate form of self-mastery for the win.

## D = Decision-Makers

Coaches are the ultimate decision-makers for strategies, tactics, player lineups and rotations, and practice plans. Coaches with a clear vision provide purpose and direction to their staff, the TAT members, parents, and athletes. Most humans feel inspired by a compelling vision, which results in them giving their best team efforts.

Athlete involvement in decision-making may vary depending on the coach's leadership style and the maturity and readiness of the team. Some coaching staffs may grant more autonomy to experienced players, particularly with on-field decision-making.

Autocratic coaches make decisions unilaterally, with little to no input from the athletes. Communication is direct, and athletes are expected to follow directions without question or pushback. These coaches make the decisions because they have the best vantage point in knowing the ins and outs of their team, the opponent, and the game. Democratic leadership, in contrast, values athletes' input, as their opinions and preferences could influence the successful execution of the game plan. Reaching consensus via team discussions can encourage greater buy-in, a sense of team cohesion and ownership, and increased player empowerment.

A leaderless or flat leadership style that is more laissez-faire relies heavily on player autonomy, creativity, and initiative to make decisions. However, having less structure may lead to more disorganization and frustration unless the players are emotionally ready and experienced enough to organize themselves. Athletes may first need some practice and guidance with question-based coaching so they can mature into handling practice and training more independently.

A famous non-sport example of leaderless leadership is a conductorless orchestra whose members learn to carefully listen to and tune in to the music-making of others. This type of structure results in a highly collaborative process of shared responsibility that allows for innovation and creativity that might not be present with a conductor.

There is no coaching leadership style that is objectively optimal, as the best style is the one that brings out the best in each athlete, as well as in the team collectively. Knowing who you are and who your athletes are is the starting place for impactful leadership, regardless of the style used. Tuning in to and listening to the athletes with flexibility and adaptability allows the coach to know when to push and when to back off, increasing the chances of success for the individual contributor and the collective team. A coach's openness, curiosity, and willingness to always be learning will sustain a lifelong career of satisfaction in coaching and the likelihood of producing winning teams.

# TAT (GROWS)

TAT members, a diverse group of professionals, collectively serve as guardians of the guardrails. This team—comprising athletic directors, administrators, and performance specialists such as sports medicine physicians, athletic trainers, physical therapists, S&C coaches, sports scientists, nutritionists, sports psychologists and mental performance coaches, academic advisors, and other support roles—is dedicated to the welfare of athletes.

## *G = Guardians of the guardrails*

Guardians protect the guardrails, which consist of the safety, ethical, and moral boundaries set by the sport's organizational and governing bodies and by the organizations that license practitioners who work with and treat athletes. Guardrails are organizational values, culture, rules, policies, and procedures put in place to protect the safety and welfare of the athletes. TAT members, as proactive guardians, work to prevent instances of physical, sexual, mental, and emotional abuse of athletes, learning from infamous cases such as Jerry Sandusky at Penn State; the Maryland football coach who verbally abused a player during a hot summer training session in which the athlete died of a heatstroke; and the criminal behavior of Larry Nassar, former USA women's national gymnastics team and Michigan State sports physician.

National, state, and local sports organizations and their governing bodies put in place both mandated and self-initiated policies after countless athletes have come forward to report their experiences of abuse. The US Center for SafeSport, the NCAA Board of Governors Policy on Campus Sexual Violence, and legislation such as the Protecting Young Victims from Sexual Abuse and Safe Sport Authorization Act of 2018, alongside required safety and welfare training for any staff members with direct access to athletes, are all steps in the right direction. Legislation has helped create safer environments for athletes, where their rights and overall well-being are prioritized.

Some universities have separated sports medicine and mental health providers from their athletic departments so that health professionals can make objective decisions without having pressures or biases from coaches or athletes who may want athletes to continue playing through injury. However, the roles of TAT members in being on the front lines of protecting the safety, health, and welfare of athletes for both short-term and long-term outcomes cannot be overstated. TAT members are armed with performance, health, and wellness expertise. Ethical, moral, and legal standards are their guardrails, and they make the final decisions about athlete availability, always guarding their safety, health, and overall protection.

## R = Resource extender

A resource extender is someone with knowledge of resources outside their own expertise that can help an athlete. Resources might include referrals to other performance and health specialists, specialists in financial or legal aid, housing assistance, academic advising, and family or relationship support. A trusting relationship with a TAT member can help an athlete deal with life stressors outside the athletic arena. If they do not know the answers themselves, TAT members often go above and beyond to connect an athlete to resources that are available beyond the scope of just athletics.

## O = Obstacle remover

An obstacle remover can assist an athlete in removing unnecessary obstacles that do not serve a greater purpose. For example, TAT members have sometimes supported athletes in successfully and ethically taking academic exams while they were traveling for games by working with the professors on making such accommodations. Other examples might include helping an athlete obtain to-go meals at dining facilities after training or before heading to class. TAT members are dedicated to facilitating access to resources that promote the welfare of athletes per their unique needs, making athletes feel supported and cared for.

## W = Warranter

A warranter is someone who authorizes, affirms, or permits an action, legislation or policy, financial investment, or similar event to take place. Without sports administrators guiding the culture, values, policies, and procedures, some athletic environments might resemble the Wild West. Warranters approve which behaviors are okay or not okay by helping to set and enforce the guardrails. In cases of abuse, athlete welfare was not the priority of administrators who cared more about the reputation and brand of their institution. TAT members are responsible for enforcing rules and policies for safety and for speaking up to protect athletes from abuse. Warranters also direct resources such as financial support to hire good people to care for and improve facilities, equipment, and technology to create optimal ecosystems wherein athletes, coaches, and spectators can thrive.

## S = Safety and Prevention

TAT members coach, support, advise, and guide athletes in the knowledge, attitudes, and behaviors of safe and healthy performance. They are committed to ensuring that athletes get proper sleep and recovery time; nutritious diets and adequate hydration; practice proper form and biomechanics; utilize periodization and progression in strength and conditioning that prevents overtraining; and execute proper techniques in injury prehab and rehab routines. They also use sports science metrics to track, manage, and report the cognitive, emotional, and physical load of athletes, which informs their training plans, and they help manage athletes' social, mental, and emotional wellness so they can perform at their best. TAT members work as a unified team to help prevent injury and illness, treat and rehabilitate injuries, and prepare athletes to be healthy, available, and ready for the competition arena, instilling confidence and security in the system.

## Giving and Receiving Feedback: A Continuum

Growing and developing involves being able to give and receive feedback to make the system or the part even better. Feedback isn't just about approval, although that's important, as it helps us understand what's working and where we're succeeding. Encouragement provides support and builds momentum to keep us on track. To accelerate progress, we need to learn from others what needs improvement and how our behavior or attitudes affect others, especially when we lack awareness in these areas. We may be blind to our own latent talent, skills, and knowledge that others can inspire and bring forth in us.

People differ in how much criticism, feedback, and directness they prefer. The "tell it like it is" approach doesn't work for everyone. Some may want a softer, more encouraging approach with pats on the back, praise, and kinder suggestions on how to make corrections. Effective feedback strikes a balance—providing both praise and constructive criticism to reassure and guide athletes in their development.

The feedback continuum ranges from praise and encouragement to direct criticism. Consider the feedback continuum before offering coaching to system members. Athletes benefit most when they share where they fall on the continuum of feedback, helping teammates and coaches communicate more effectively and work better together. Simply asking people where they fall on the continuum or doing an activity called the feedback lineup are valuable approaches to learning how people want feedback.

At IMG Academy, we used the feedback lineup to help teams understand each other. In a mental conditioning session, we marked two anchor points—encouragement and direct criticism/give-it-to-me-straight—on either side of the room or field. We then asked athletes to position themselves along an imaginary line between the two. Some placed themselves on the extreme, while others placed themselves somewhere in the middle or leaned toward one side of the continuum. Athletes had a good time seeing where each other self-selected and then having the chance to disagree and place teammates where they thought their teammates fit on the continuum. By discussing feedback and how athletes are able to best receive it allows team members and coaches to get on the same page by treating people fairly and how they like feedback, but not treat everyone the same.

Tara VanDerveer, one of the most winning coaches in NCAA history with Stanford University's women's basketball team, and who was inducted into the Women's Basketball Hall of Fame in 2002, offers excellent examples of giving potent feedback. You might use a similar approach to Coach VanDerveer's when a player is struggling with their performance and complaining about not playing or starting. The athlete may want to blame the coaches for this, but by acknowledging the player's frustration and being open and curious with the athlete to help them reflect on their own actions, the coach can help the player take more ownership of their performance and identify areas for improvement.

One day a first-year student, who was one of the nation's most highly-recruited athletes, flopped herself onto Coach VanDerveer's office couch and stated, "Coach, I'm mad. I'm barely getting any playing time. I have always started and played every minute. I need to get into the game more." Coach VanDerveer paused and responded, "You know what? I'm mad, too! I think you should be getting more playing time, too. Why do you think you are not getting more playing time?" Surprised by Coach VanDerveer's response, the student-athlete considered the question. She paused, too. Her facial expression changed from upset and angry to curious and open. "Maybe because sometimes I'm late for practice and can be lazy. I need to work harder in practice and on defense. Also, I need to improve my fitness." Coach nodded, encouraging her student-athlete's reflection. "What else can you improve to get more playing time?"

"Well, I guess my attitude could be better. I have focused on myself and have not been very team-oriented. I guess I have some work to do," the athlete responded. "Great talk, Coach," she joked, and popped off the sofa, excited about knowing what she needed to do. This athlete's response is a testament to the power of self-reflection in the feedback process. Her realization that her attitude and team orientation could be better demonstrates how feedback can empower athletes to take responsibility for their own growth and development.

"Nice reflection. We are here to help you. Let us know if you want to do any individual work or film review. What else is going on that you want to talk about? How's school going? Is your Biology of the Brain class going any better? How is your aunt feeling after ankle surgery?" Coach VanDerveer's open communication style fostered a sense of connection and understanding. By asking about the athlete's school and personal life, Coach VanDerveer demonstrated valuing the athlete as a whole person, not just as a player. "Yes, Coach, classes are good. The tutor has helped a lot, and my aunt has started PT. Thanks for asking. OK, I gotta get to class. See you at practice with a new attitude, and I'll be busting my butt on defense. You will not even know what to do with me! Thanks again," the athlete replied.

What do you think Coach VanDerveer did well? Why did this situation not turn into a typical coach-player conversation around playing time? Typical discussions do not include players reflecting on what they are doing well, what they could improve, and how they will help themselves improve. Instead, it often turns into a blame game on the coach for starting certain players and whining from the athlete about how hard they are working and that they deserve more playing time than others. Coach VanDerveer showed empathy by empathizing and agreeing with the athlete's feelings of anger. She asked simple questions to get the athlete to reflect on her role and responsibilities and what she could do better to earn more playing time. The coach naturally shifted the topic to the player, having the athlete identify why she thought she was not getting more playing time. The focus of the conversation became the attitude and work ethic in practice sessions, which are both within the athlete's control.

I encourage coaches to ask athletes who they should start over or replace for playing time. The coach might ask with open curiosity, "Who should I take off the field or out of the lineup to put you in?" Often, the athlete recognizes that they are less reliable or consistent than other athletes who play more. Their answer helps coaches understand the athlete's thinking and opens the conversation for the coach to share what the athlete is doing well and what the coach needs to see more or less of from their performance.

In particular situations, the coach may have a specific lineup because of what the opponents present, which may have nothing to do with how good the players on the bench are. Upfront conversations help to mitigate hostile questioning, doubt, and confusion in athletes who may perceive lineup changes as unfair. Coaches who play favorites, don't give certain athletes a chance for biased or unfair reasons, or use playing time and starting lineups in toxic ways should examine the impacts of their choices on the team's environment of trust. Gaslighting is a manipulation tactic that a coach may use to convince an athlete that their understanding of reality is invalid, which results in distrust, confusion, and poor performance. From a sports psychologist's point of view, the more that a coach is curious and open and leads with effective questions posed to the athlete to seek understanding, the more the athlete has a chance to reflect, get curious, and shift their focus from the blame-and-complain game to playing the Game of self-mastery and confidence ownership.

In turn, athletes must understand that coaches have the remit of winning games, providing positive sporting experiences, and taking care of their athletes. Taking care of the athlete includes being honest about where athletes stand in their development, progress, and playing in competitions. The athlete can thereby feel empowered about their decision to either stay on the team, figure it out, compete, or find another program that is a better fit. The athlete must understand that they take themselves wherever they go, so they need to learn what they have to do better when it comes to practicing, contributing positively, competing, being a team member, accepting criticism and feedback, and affecting relationship dynamics.

## Make a Pact

A pact is a commitment or promise between people to maintain responsibility for playing their role in supporting the common goal of the system, which is to create positive sporting experiences. In an orchestra, each musician plays specific notes and maintains a synchronized rhythm, volume, tenor, and timing so the performance can succeed in its goal of creating beautiful music for the audience. In contrast, solely thinking about oneself and one's own goals makes it more challenging to be in sync with others.

A rowing team is a great example of a winning pact or system: When the oars of one rower are even slightly off from their alignment with the others, the boat's forward momentum is not nearly as fast or efficient. In order to win regattas and championships, everyone on the team has to accept their role and row to the best of their ability without complaining about which seat they're in. If a single team member is out of sorts, the whole boat may careen.

Conversely, it is uncomfortable, chaotic, and unpleasant for everyone when even just one team member is off. If a parent, coach, or athlete was part of a rowing team and stuck their oar in the water with poor timing, being out of sync with the other members of the system, it would rock the whole boat. In crew, no single rower or role matters more than the others. All of them matter equally and contribute to the success of the boat.

Parents should take their roles just as seriously as the players and coaches do and understand that they can throw a system off by sticking their oars in the water at the wrong time. There is a time and place to speak up if something dysfunctional occurs within a system, and failure to adhere to these guidelines may result in poor sporting experiences, disruptions, and unnecessary suffering.

Making a written agreement can be very helpful for clearly spelling out what behaviors, responsibilities, and expectations all members of the system want to agree upon. A sample agreement is available in the appendix, which you can feel free to adapt to the needs of your organization. PACT members can sign the pact, agreeing to fulfill their responsibilities and play their roles well.

# CHAPTER 5

# What Is the Strategy?

Now that you understand the rules and roles, let's talk strategy, which is the Confident Performer model. This model establishes a strong foundation for lifelong mental health and performance. The confident performer rises from attaining a solid Human-First identity and then becoming a whole-person and healthy performer. The mental skills that focus on performance are at the top of the model. Hence, it is important at the first tier to invest the most effort in your identity development as a Human-First.

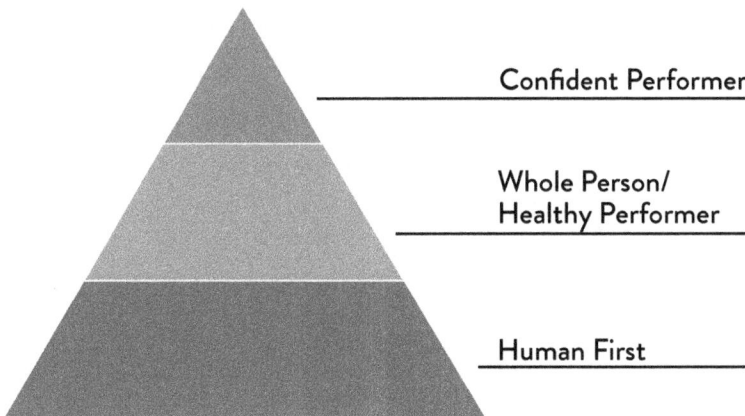

Confident Performer

Whole Person/
Healthy Performer

Human First

## The Confidence Ownership Model

Identifying as a Human-First is foundational to your success in self-mastery and confidence ownership. If you were to skip the foundational build-out of your Human-First identity and jump into developing the skills of a confident performer, you would risk leaving gaps and ending up with a wobbly foundation. A Human-First identity helps you develop protective factors for your mental, emotional, physical, and spiritual health and performance, centering you on humanity and natural intelligence. When you have built a solid foundation on which you stand confidently, you won't fall as far when a poor performance happens and you will bounce back more quickly from mental, physical, or emotional injuries.

Without a Human-First identity, people can get too caught up in overidentifying with their role identity, such as being an athlete, parent, coach, or TAT member. Your primary responsibilities as a human on planet Earth are first to survive (which includes needs such as breathing, food, water, shelter, and sleep), then to maintain your health (including organ, cellular, and musculoskeletal functions), and then to cultivate social groups (meeting the needs of education, protection, safety, and belongingness). Similarly, in 1943 the psychologist Abraham Maslow identified five categories of human needs in his hierarchy of needs model: physiological, safety and security, love and belonging, self-esteem, and self-actualization.[11] To live a flourishing, thriving, self-actualized life and be a consistent and confident performer, embracing your Human-First identity helps you maintain a sense of perspective with performance, which happens in a distinct and finite period of time.

Individuals whose primary or only identity is being an athlete, parent, or coach tend to run into mental health and performance challenges when things don't go well in those arenas. Michael Phelps, the world's most decorated Olympic swimmer, stated that when he solely viewed himself as an athlete, he felt more depressed. Maintaining the complexities of being a human while playing a specific role in a winning system results in better mental health outcomes and a more balanced perspective on your performances, allowing you to maintain motivation for pursuing excellence in other areas of your life as well.

Developing your Human-First identity involves deep self-awareness and a willingness to examine your natural tendencies, learned behaviors, core values, and best attributes. One way to support this exploration is to utilize personality assessments such as the Myers-Briggs Type Indicator, the DISC (Dominance, Influence, Steadiness, and Compliance) model, and the California Personality Inventory (CPI), which can help with expanding self-awareness. You can also journal about your strengths, areas of growth, and favorite characteristics, keeping in mind the attributes other people have said you possess. Ask trustworthy sources for feedback on both your strengths and areas of improvement and reflect on past successes as well as situations that did not work in your favor. Aim to understand what characteristics you possess when you're at your best in the four major life domains: leader-self, role (parent, athlete, coach, or TAT), work or school, and relationships. I invite you to do more profound work to understand the sources of your identity, which include your life force, human beingness, genetics, learning experiences, trauma responses, affiliations and influences, and choices. When you draw on your predispositions, strengths, and areas of improvement, your Choice Identities will be more meaningful and more aligned with how you are wired. Choice Identities will be explained further in Chapter 12. Your awareness will be grounded in reality, not based on fantasies or on who someone else wants you to be.

The middle section of the model, whole-person/healthy performer, focuses on the six fundamentals of a healthy performer and well-balanced human. These skills will be covered in more depth in Section 3. Essentially the healthier you are in mind, body, emotions, and spirit, the better you perform, the more likely you are to prevent physical or emotional injury, and the faster you will recover from any type of injury.

The final component of the model is the confident performer, which consists of the mental skills with which most, if not all, elite and professional athletes are familiar. Athletes utilize these skills when the pressure is on, either consciously or unconsciously, to be at their best. These skills can help you close the gap between where you are and where you want to be in your Choice Identities within the four life domains. Most sports psychologists only teach their athletes to improve their core mental skills for sustaining high performance. Unfortunately, I have found that without the depth of work I offer here, even mental skills don't seem to help when you need them the most.

As your self-awareness expands and your circumstances change, the confident performer model can be adapted to evolve with you. I designed the model to help simplify the complexities of adjusting to the needs of the moment. The greatest exemplars of self-mastery are people who show up intentionally based on a deep understanding of who they are and what they want. They adapt to other people and to their circumstances, offering their best self so they can be responsive to creating the optimal outcomes for all.

## You Are More than Your Sport or Your Role

Athletes who have the most difficult time dealing with loss, injury, transition, or retirement from sport tend to identify almost exclusively with their primary identity as being an athlete, having placed minimal emphasis or value on developing their other identities outside of involvement in their sport. When something goes wrong in their athletic life, their whole world feels wobbly because their self-worth, self-esteem, and confidence have been derived exclusively from performing well and achieving as an athlete. The same can be said for an overly-identified parent, coach or TAT member. The adjustment to unexpected outcomes, transitions to new roles and identities, or loss of identity can be equally difficult when other identities are underdeveloped.

Understandably, professional or Olympic athletes may have a robust identity as athletes, which drives the behaviors that put them at the top of their game. To perform at a high-quality level day after day, a world-class athlete must invest a great deal of time in taking care of their body with proper sleep, fueling, and hydration; having deliberate, focused training sessions; receiving coaching and feedback; doing recovery sessions such as massage and ice baths; and maintaining mental training to keep their minds sharp. When someone invests exorbitant amounts of time, effort, and resources into maintaining a particular identity, it becomes easy to overidentify with it.

This phenomenon isn't limited to athletes; other high performers also tend to define themselves primarily by one role. Great performers have a strong sense of who they are in their performance domain and likely focus on that role as their primary identity. Even in other fields, like comedy, high performers like Jerry Seinfeld and Chris Rock have stated that their primary identity is a comedian, not actor, parent, producer, celebrity, or any other role. Although they are more than just comedians, as they are humans first, their strong work identity is what propels them to reach their levels of comedic genius.

An overidentification with any of your identities can be problematic because other facets of your life can become underdeveloped. For example, you may overidentify with being a parent as your priority and your primary role in life. The benefits of having a strong identity as a parent include doing a good job of looking out for your child's well-being, keeping your child safe from harm and danger, and providing countless educational and experiential opportunities for your child to develop, grow, and thrive. However, being overly identified as a parent may mean that when your child is having a difficult time, you do everything in your power to take that pain away, which may inadvertently take away your child's opportunities to develop skills of resiliency and emotional fortitude.

Because different identities may require varying levels of attention at different times, learning how to navigate these shifts is key. One identity might need more of your attention, focus, and effort at certain times. When you perform poorly in one identity, you can use your other identities to help bolster your confidence, rebound, and propel the identity that needs to be worked on to greater heights.

A failure to perform does not make you a failure as a person. Remember you are more than just one role. Parents, coaches, TAT members, and athletes—your value extends beyond your title. Maintaining perspective that you are a human first helps you connect with common humanity and reconnect with yourself during hardship. Developing each identity with specific virtues and behaviors allows you to show up as the better to best possible version of yourself, no matter the role.

## How Most Performers Train: Upside Down Model

Athletes, what if you focused all your waking moments on your sports performance? Parents, coaches, or TAT members, what if you focused all your energy solely on the performance of your role identity? It would be like flipping the confidence ownership model upside down. Very little time would be invested in your Human-First identities, resulting in the point of the triangle becoming an unstable foundation. The largest area of the triangle would become about performance, even outside of the performance arena. Placing too much emphasis on being a confident performer would result in your Human-First foundation being underdeveloped, which destabilizes the whole system. When suboptimal performances happen, despite exceptional planning and preparation, performers with a weak Human-First identity would fall further because they have a wobbly base that lacks the foundation to help them bounce back up. They would also likely stay down longer and face a more treacherous path to clawing their way back to the top.

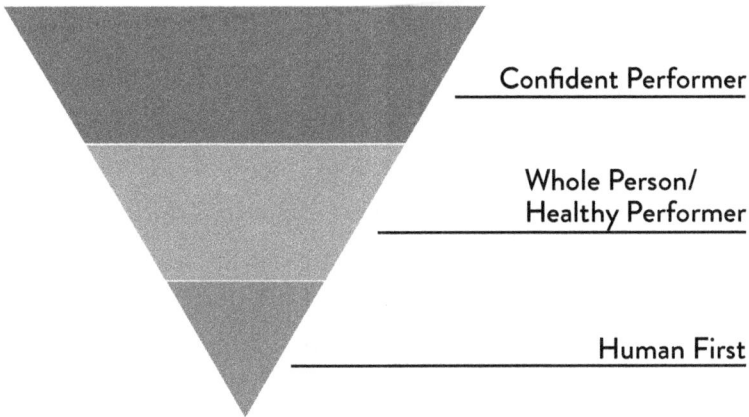

- Confident Performer
- Whole Person/ Healthy Performer
- Human First

## *The Upside Down Confidence Ownership Model*

This theoretical model came to life in a real-world scenario at a prestigious university's volleyball team that worked for a year to turn around the mental health and performance outcomes of their student-athletes. The team's performance had declined over the past several years, with high levels of stress and anxiety being reported among the athletes. The team had talent but was not meeting expectations for winning games and championships. The student-athletes struggled with confidence issues, and the coaching staff had a high turnover rate. They were known for being the "problem team" in the university's athletic department, and alumni began pressuring the athletic director to improve the team's results and reduce complaints. The athletic director hired a sports psychologist to implement the confidence ownership model for the volleyball team, which focused on helping the student-athletes and coaches to develop a strong sense of their Choice Identities, personal values and goals, and team values and goals, thereby bolstering their confidence by improving their mental skills on and off the court.

The student-athletes participated in biweekly sessions that served as a platform for self-reflection. These sessions were not just about assessing the athletes' personality types or identifying their core values, but about delving deep into their identities and understanding how these values and attributes translated into their actions. Coaches were also part of this journey, having been trained in the same model to work on their own identities and to positively and authentically reinforce the athletes' self-identified values and goals. The team engaged in confident performer exercises and discussions to foster a more supportive culture and develop a common language. They were encouraged to discuss what they were learning with their parents so that the parents would also be on board with the progress of the mental health and performance program. Athletes were encouraged to set performance goals that were aligned with their values and identities rather than defining success based only on the amount of personal playing time, their stats, or winning games. This emphasis on self-reflection was not just a tool for performance improvement, but a journey of personal growth and self-discovery.

Within a single season, the volleyball team's performance saw a remarkable improvement, with many student-athletes achieving personal best in both individual and team stats. The team's focus on the process, rather than on the outcomes, paid off. They clinched their league championship, a feat they hadn't accomplished in the previous five years. The satisfaction of the student-athletes soared, and the athletic department received fewer complaints about the coaching staff. The athletic director, too, experienced a renewed sense of job satisfaction and confidence in their leadership. The success of the confident performer program was evident, as the university's volleyball team went on to have winning seasons. The student-athletes subsequently graduated with the skills of confident performers that they could successfully apply in all aspects of their lives.

# SECTION 2

## Getting to Know Your Selves

# Chapter 6

# Who Are You?

"Who am I? Who are you? Who are we?" These are the age-old questions that philosophers, professors, scientists, neurologists, psychiatrists, psychologists, religious and spiritual leaders, and humans from every walk of life have asked themselves because how you answer this question impacts how your life path will unfold. Perhaps you have also asked yourself, "Who am I?" in the past, or perhaps other people have asked you in either a personal or professional setting to tell them about yourself. How you answer that question often depends on the context.

Let's take a closer look at what identity means and how it's shaped, as this helps you discern what makes you uniquely yourself. Identity is deeply personal and includes your beliefs, values, self-concept, specific attributes and values. In sum, identity is self-defined and is centered on how individuals view themselves and their place in the world. Awareness of what makes you who you are when you are at your best helps provide the confidence to enter new circumstances with greater ease; is crucial for becoming the confident, consistent performer you want to be; and is the fundamental question in building the foundation of your mental health and performance. What behaviors and choices do you want to enhance in your Choice Identities? Embrace that you are multifaceted and unique and only you get to be you in the world. In essence, you consist of multiple identities, and in this chapter, we will look at the four main sources of identities and how they relate to building this foundation.

When you ask yourself, "Who am I?" you may think of various dimensions of the self. You might fill in the blank after the words "I am ..." by answering with your full name, age, what you do, including one or more of your roles, your nationality, or your gender. But are these descriptors truly who you are? Likewise, I could answer the question by saying, "I am Andrea Wieland (my full name, which may imply my sociocultural identity). I am a psychologist (my work role). I am an athlete (my role and energy identity). I am a dog and horse owner (which reflects my values about animals). I am an extension and reflection of natural intelligence and universal energy (my human identity)." These examples reflect how I see myself.

Who are you currently in relation to your goals, and who must you become as new opportunities present themselves? As forks in the road emerge and various people flow in and out of your life over time, how do your experiences inform who you are and who you want to work toward becoming? Your view of yourself in relation to your goals has important implications for what you will achieve and how you persist in bouncing back from setbacks and challenges. How you handle the inevitable disappointments and hardships you will face depends on how you see yourself, what your beliefs are, and what kind of person you think you are.

When you have a game plan that's focused on self-mastery, dealing with adversity can strengthen your sense of self and increase your skillful means for handling more significant and complex challenges. Without developing those skills, you may feel like you are being tossed around at sea while only wearing a life jacket. To forge a deeper understanding of who we are, develop compassion for others, develop the skillful means to reach our highest potential, and live a satisfying and meaningful life as we pursue our most important goals, we must seek, face, and embrace challenges. My hope is that your growth from playing the self-mastery Game will not only help you win more sports games, but will also help you develop into a leader who can lend a hand, heart, and brain to solving the most relevant and impactful challenges you, others, and our planet face, and to helping others become the best versions of themselves.

## Basic Purpose of Life

Becoming the full expression of who you are is the most basic purpose in life. Extraordinary humans naturally produce exceptional results, and you will too when you focus on remembering that you already are extraordinary. The world needs you to offer your best self, and if you accept that premise, your identities will evolve to meet the demands of today and what your future best selves require of you. Playing the right game starts with who you are today, who you believe yourself to be, and who you intend to be. These are all predicated on your beliefs, assumptions, goals, what you believe is possible for yourself, and the types of people you affiliate with. How would you complete the following sentences concerning who you believe yourself to be today and what you think is possible for you?

- "I'm the kind of person who ..."
- "What my present and future holds for me are ..."
- "My primary purpose is ..."
- "What and who I hold to be most dear are ..."
- "My future Self needs me to ..."
- "My accomplishments in the next year, 3 years, 5 years, and 10 years will include ..."
- "What I tell myself about my past, other people, and situations that make me feel confident is ..."

- "What I tell myself about my past, other people, and situations that make me feel discouraged is ..."
- "How I might instead see the discouraging parts as serving to grow my confidence instead of tearing it down is ..."

Your answers to these questions will evolve as you learn more about yourself over time. These answers may help you recognize your virtues and values, which are the essence of who you are, who you want to be, and who your future self needs you to be in order to reach your non-negotiable goals. Knowing who you are and how you want to show up in various situations and with particular people provides you with stability and confidence for choosing your responses, serving as the foundation of your mental health and performance.

## What Are Identities?

Identity is your sense of self, and it consists of virtues, attributes, behaviors, and beliefs. It is important to understand your foundational human identity, unique character patterns and tendencies, sociocultural identities, and shadow sides (known as "parts" in Internal Family Systems language). I will share a method for consciously selecting your virtues, values, and targeted behaviors in your Choice Identities in four significant areas of life.

The very bases of what and how you think, act, feel, and make decisions; what you believe to be true or not; what your attitudes are about any number of people, places, and things; and how you interact with others and your environment all depend on your Self-Identity. The most successful goal achievers and life impactors are conscious about who they are and intend to be, whereas other people run on autopilot, unaware of how much choice they have. Behaving in ways that are beyond your sense of who you believe yourself to be tends to be rare. Ecosystems, environments, other people, and genetics have an influence over who you become. Of course, there are circumstances when you may behave outside of your usual tendencies. Typically though, identities change because of conscious and repeated choices or being under the influence of a state-altering substance(s), or after a life-altering event.

The four primary sources of identity that inform your Choice Identities are:

- human identity
  - common humanity
  - universal energy
  - life force
  - vital energy
  - loving awareness
  - source energy
  - natural intelligence
  - inner being
- personality type
  - unique patterns and tendencies that are learned or genetically determined (see link to Myers-Briggs Type Indicators assessment in Appendix B)
- sociocultural identities
  - represented by the ADDRESSING model by Pamela Hays, which is an acronym for identities related to power that are often beyond an individual's control.[12]
- Saboteurs
  - shadow side(s), subpersonalities from prolonged "negative" emotions that sabotage one's mental well-being as described in the positive intelligence theory by Shirzad Chamine[13]
  - can be interchanged with "parts" from Internal Family Systems Theory (IFS)

Each of these will be discussed in more depth in chapters 7–10. These four primary sources of identity are enacted at the unconscious or subconscious levels. Active therapeutic work, guidance, or specialized coaching can help with examining how all the sources of identities work together. I recommend that you work on understanding yourself from the perspective of these four sources. How have your experiences informed who you are? How has trauma affected how you see yourself? What have your sociocultural identities enabled you to do or not do? In what areas of your life might you be limited or believe that you are limited because someone else told you so? How have your beliefs helped you or hindered your life experiences so far?

Consider your unique patterns and tendencies. When you read your profile from a personality assessment, you might say, "Yes, that is like me!" Examine each sociocultural identity individually and be curious about how you identify. How has that sociocultural identity dimension influenced how you see yourself, with whom you affiliate, and your beliefs because of how you relate to that identity? Contrast your identities with those of someone who identifies differently than you. We may make assumptions based on what we see as being salient to others' identities, which may or may not be the case. How would you feel if others assumed something about you that is not true for you?

## *The four sources of identities to inform your Choice Identities*

The multiplicity of personality theory, first postulated by one of the "fathers of psychology," William James, in 1890, states that we have multiple versions of ourselves that arise depending on the social situation.[14] You may have thought, "A part of me wants to do this, and a part of me wants to do that." This is a perfectly normal and common experience. The theory reminds us that having multiple aspects of ourselves is a healthy response to an ever-changing, fast-paced world, allowing us greater flexibility across different contexts.

Yet, the unified theory of self and personality states that we have one single personality that applies to all situations.[15] [16] [17] According to this view, we are the same person at work or school as we are at home, in intimate relationships, with friends, in the competitive arena, or at the grocery store. For example, Trait Theory states that the Big Five personality traits (neuroticism, extraversion, openness, agreeableness, and conscientiousness) are mostly stable traits over time and situations. The Biological Basis of Personality theory purports that genetic underpinnings shape how core traits express themselves consistently over time and space. Longitudinal studies show that while personality can evolve and mature, core traits tend to remain stable.[18] I believe that many individuals who haven't explored their sense of self might assume they possess a single, unified personality. This assumption can lead to confusion when they say or do something that doesn't align with their self-perception.

My preference is for the multiplicity of self that allows for flexibility and adaptability to people, circumstances, and events. You likely have core values, attributes, and behaviors that are expressed due to genetics, environmental factors, learning, experiences, trauma, and what the situation, people, and circumstances bring out in you. When you think about the different people, circumstances, and events you've encountered, were you the same person every time, or did the context dynamics bring out your various attitudes, behaviors, virtues, and values? As we walk through the identity section of the confident performer model, you may agree that the multiplicity of self theory makes the most sense. Being able to recognize which of your identities is the best one to bring to a specific situation does not mean that you are not being yourself, but rather that you have multiple selves to optimally choose from.

Understanding the four sources of identities in the confident performer model can help you develop your Choice Identities in the four primary life domains. Each source offers a comprehensive understanding of who you are, why you value what you value, why you act the way you do, think the way you think, and respond the way you respond. This understanding can empower you to make conscious decisions about your attributes and behaviors and help you break free from the notion that you are stuck with your genetic predisposition and learned behavior. Past behaviors do not always predict future behavior, and you have the extraordinary opportunity to choose and change.

## Parts

We all have parts of ourselves that we may not particularly like or that get in the way when we are on the brink of a breakthrough. These Saboteur parts of ourselves, which develop from trauma experiences that typically occur in childhood, are well-intentioned protectors but often do a horrible job of helping us get what we want. Understanding the part's good intentions will help us befriend, be curious about, and listen to how the part is trying to help. This will better allow the part to support the internal system. If we help our darker sides come into the light, they are less likely to sabotage our positive efforts at the wrong moments. For more information, I encourage you to explore the books and training materials offered by the IFS Institute, which was founded by Dr. Richard Schwartz, who is the creator of the IFS model.

You can use what you have learned about characteristics, values, and virtues from the four sources of identities to formulate your Choice Identities for who you want to be in the four life domains of self-leader, role, work or school, and relationships. Nature and nurture (genetics and learning) make up much of who we are, but we are not confined to those influences alone. We have a choice of who we want to be in each moment when we consciously decide to enact our best qualities, virtues, and values. You can own your confidence as you hone your ability to respond with your best characteristics, intentions, and most precious goals.

## Influences and Drivers of Identity Development: Nature, Nurture, Affiliation, Trauma and Choice

Identity development is a complex, expansive, and intricate field of study because it is challenging to disentangle the sources of influence and drivers of why you became who you are today and who you will be in the future. My theory is that identity development is influenced by five primary drivers:

- Nature
  - o DNA and genetics
  - o you are part of the human species (as opposed to another mammal species)
  - o life force (you have life force within you that moves, breathes, and evolves)
- Nurture
  - o environmental factors
  - o opportunities afforded by context, education, application, and repetition
- Affiliation
  - o mentors and exemplars
  - o influences
  - o peers and social circles
  - o sociocultural factors
- Trauma experiences
  - o abuse or neglect
  - o chronic shame
  - o bullying or harassment
  - o accidents and natural disasters

- o   war, combat, or conflict
- o   loss of a loved one
- o   witnessing violence
- Choice
  - o   intentions
  - o   chosen behavior and decisions

Nature plays a significant role in identity development, starting from the fact that you were born with the genetic predisposition of being a human, which is rather fantastic. We all have unique genotypes, the combination of our DNA inherited from our great ancestors to our present-day biological parents, such as the color of our eyes. We also have phenotypes, which is how our genetic predisposition is expressed, and per the field of epigenetics, we have dormant genes that get switched on or off due to our own lifestyle choices, as well as those of our parents and ancestors. For example, your mother may have (had) a genetic predisposition for being an athlete, a leader, or a caring person who wants to nurture athletes, and her choice of pursuing athletics (environmental opportunities) allows you to now express those genetic predispositions from your mom turning on her athletic genes due to environmental opportunities. You were born with unique strengths, gifts, talents, and capabilities that you can further hone and activate depending on your environment!

You may wish to ask your parent(s) what you were like between ages zero and three. Was your personality during your early childhood similar to how you are today? I have one picture of myself at age two or three that represents a large part of my personality that has repeatedly been evident in my life since. In the picture, I am in a one-piece navy-blue swimsuit on a beach, enthusiastically running toward my mother with a giant laughing smile. Much like today, I charge forward enthusiastically, expecting the best from myself and others, and with a smile on my face. What's the childhood photo that most represents who you are at your core?

Nurture or environmental influences, such as all the resources and parameters around you, turn on certain aspects of your gene expression as you develop. Your environment includes the people with whom you affiliate, such as family members, classmates, teammates, coaches, mentors, exemplars, and teachers, who all play roles in your development. Suppose you had little to zero genetic predisposition toward sports, very few opportunities for getting involved in athletics in the area where you grew up, and no one encouraging you to go out for sports. In this scenario, the likelihood of you even having an interest in sports is slim to none, because your affiliations and the opportunities you are given impact your views of the world. Ultimately, you decided to take part in sports. You have chosen to be involved with and pursue athletically related goals. You may have never developed your athletic potential without the influences of the people and opportunities around you.

# Chapter 7

# The Foundational Source of Identities: Natural Intelligence

Most if not all the greatest athletes of all time know and dedicate themselves to diligent work and paying attention to the fundamentals. Kobe Bryant was known for already being at the gym at 4:30 AM, sweating, and ready to work relentlessly and diligently on his fundamentals. He was not working on 360-degree dunks or other showboating moves, but rather Bryant was working on what made him great: his ball-handling and consistency in shooting. "The Black Mamba" was his basketball identity, also known as his alter ego because when he played, he wanted to be fast, smooth, and lethal.

So, what makes you great? Start with being human and remembering that we are humans first before all other identities. In our overscheduled, stimuli-bombarded lifestyles, this may be easy to forget that we are humans first, especially when pursuing our most significant goals. We might be over-identified with any number of roles we play. When asked who you are, you might have a very narrow answer such as, "I'm a parent," or "I'm a student-athlete," or "I'm a coach." Those are roles, but do not foundationally describe who you are.

If you began identifying as being human first, how would you react to disappointing situations such as losing a game or not earning the position you want…yet? Or are you not getting the attention or promotion you think you deserve …yet? Would these be stress-inducing situations, or could your stress be reduced if you remind yourself that you are not alone in your common human experiences? You are part of the common humanity. Perhaps your stress can soften and help you keep a bigger picture in mind.

Adopting a Human-First approach allows us to hold more space and perspective for all the shared universal annoyances, frustrations, hurts, and disappointments we humans experience during our lifetimes. We have shared universal experiences that every human on the planet experiences, regardless of where on the planet. Ancient wisdom such as Taoism, Hinduism, and modern cognitive science agree that at the base of our shared human experience is natural intelligence, though its name may come in multiple forms. For ease and consistency, I will call it natural intelligence. Refer to this life energy to whatever name resonates with you (life force, Universal Energy, God, Allah, Beingness, Loving Awareness, etc.). Natural Intelligence is the same life force that grows the grass and trees, moves the animals, operates throughout the multiverse, and gives us access to greater clarity and wisdom.

## What Is Natural Intelligence, and How Does It Relate to My Identity?

Natural Intelligence is the same life force that grows the grass and trees, moves the animals, operates throughout the multiverse, and gives us access to greater clarity and wisdom. This section is by no means religious or spiritual discourse. Rather, the Human-First identity approach in the confident performer model posits that we all have a life force running through us that we are connected to, which is foundational to mental health and performance. By understanding your first human identity, you can connect to the miracle of life, and the innate joy and experience of just being alive and a human on this planet at this unique time in history.

Natural intelligence can be a benevolent source of wisdom, inspiration, clarity, and guidance for achieving your goals, making decisions, and recovering from injury or trauma as you strive to develop to your highest potential. From the perspective of natural intelligence, life is happening *for* you, not *to* you. You can access the universe's wisdom by resting with what is, knowing that natural intelligence supports all living beings and is that from which you can never be separate.

You may, at times, feel distant physically, emotionally, or relationally from people you have not yet met in your own neighborhood or from people living on the other side of the planet from you. However, quantum physics informs us that it is impossible for us to ever be separate. If there is no separation, then how is there an epidemic of loneliness and isolation?

When we feel disconnected from ourselves, not knowing our value, not knowing who we are at our core, we are more likely to feel separate and disconnected from others. When we feel alone or isolated, it is because we have forgotten the basic source of connection to the life force around us. This understanding can help us feel that we are always part of something larger and that we always belong. The more you can identify with and practice remembering your Human-First identity within the context of natural intelligence, the more ease and trust you will consistently feel, and your mental health will be more supported. In essence, you won't succumb to basic human fears including being outcast, rejected, abandoned, disrespected, ignored, or dismissed. We are social beings who need to be seen and heard and feel like we matter in order to maintain an equanimous state of mental health.

## Perfectly Imperfect

As we tap into our natural intelligence, we can feel compassion for ourselves and others for being perfectly imperfect, although it is often easier to have compassion for others than for ourselves. The dissatisfaction, non-acceptance, and intolerance we feel toward ourselves are related to our feelings of disappointment or disdain that we are imperfect. We treat our imperfections as if something is seriously wrong with us, making us feel disconnected from ourselves and others. If we cannot stand ourselves, we may wonder how others could possibly like us, let alone love us.

Accepting that we are perfectly imperfect works in progress allows us to also be more accepting of others and to feel more connected from the viewpoint of common humanity, remembering that we are all mostly experiencing similar challenges, struggles, and emotions. When we spend time in nature, rarely when we see an imperfect tree, flower, animal, or plant do we look upon it with great disdain. Considering that nature is also perfectly imperfect can be a positive step toward self-acceptance.

## The 8 Cs of the Leader-Self

A reflection of natural intelligence is tapping into your Leader-Self. Let's look at the Internal Family Systems (IFS) therapeutic model, which has had far-reaching effects on the fields of therapy and coaching. Developed by Dr. Richard Schwartz, IFS is a theory, therapy, and methodology that views the individual as being comprised of a system containing multiple parts or subpersonalities that are either working in harmony or disharmony.[19] Although some of our parts are younger or more immature, they're doing their best to serve as protectors. All parts are welcome and important, and there is no need for judgment.

Dr. Schwartz describes the Self with a capital S as inherently embodying eight universal qualities that start with the letter $c$: calm, curious, compassionate, connected, creative, clear, courageous, and confident. These qualities represent specific ways of being and relating to the world. For instance, calm refers to the ability to remain steady and composed in the face of challenges, while compassion is the capacity to empathize and care for others. These eight qualities are present when we are in our natural, relaxed states. When we are under stress or pressure, or without having education and support, certain parts that are too immature for the task at hand can take over as subpersonalities or Saboteurs.

IFS is a transformative method that has changed the lives of countless individuals seeking greater self-understanding and acceptance. By recognizing that we are comprised of a whole Self as well as its multiple parts, we can begin to discern whether we are operating from a specific part or a team of parts, or are leading from Self. Ideally, the Leader-Self harmoniously leads the other parts for optimal ease and cooperation within the system. The essential goal of IFS work is to harmonize the parts (subpersonalities) and optimize their roles so that the person can heal themselves and more effectively lead from the Self.

From my personal journey with IFS, I can testify to its transformative power. Early in my career as a psychologist, I was skeptical about whether a therapist could help me since I could tell when they were using specific techniques or trite statements; after all, I had grown up with having a psychiatrist as a father and a mother who was earning her master's in counseling psychology. I knew the arrogant part was getting in the way of benefiting from counseling, and I was having a hard time surrendering to how therapy could help me. However, I eventually had such a positive experience with IFS that I thought this approach might have a chance with others who were as stubborn and skeptical as I had been about psychotherapy! I even realized in hindsight that if I'd had the IFS tools that are designed for children when I was growing up, I might have been able to respond more effectively to difficult situations.

## What or Who is the Self?

When you're in tune with your Self or your natural intelligence, you're not trying or efforting; you're internally comfortable in your skin and responsive to external people and circumstances. The Self is the core of our being that is always calm, compassionate, and clear. The Self leads and heals the other more extreme parts of ourselves.

We all have parts of ourselves that we don't like, and we sometimes confuse them with the whole of who we are. The parts that people often loathe in themselves, such as an Inner Critic part, have good intentions to help and protect you but are often ineffective at their jobs. When couples, coaching staff, teams, and families work with their Saboteurs and parts, they develop more effective relationships as they are better able to stop blaming and shaming and can focus more on looking inward. They learn to talk for their parts rather than from their parts. When they develop compassion for those parts that are working hard, it becomes easier to have compassion for others who also have difficult parts. Instead of reacting to other people's activated parts, you can slow down and respond from your Leader-Self.

## Kintsugi Bowls

When I was around age three, a beautiful Japanese woman babysat me. My time with her was so formative that at one point I thought she was my mother. Because of her influence, I developed an affinity for Japanese art, culture, gardens, practices, and ways of being. This tale of the Kintsugi bowl has long since resonated for me as being the perfect metaphor for the beauty of perfect imperfection in the Human-First identity.

The Tale of the Broken Bowl (Adapted)

An aged ceramist named Seritsu lived in a small Japanese village at the edge of Mount Hotaka. He was known for his exquisite ceramic creations, each with delicate details inspired by the beauty of nature surrounding his studio. As the end of the day drew near, Seritsu was finishing his meticulous work on a precious tea kettle. As he reached for his glass of water, his elbow accidentally knocked the almost finished kettle from the table, shattering it into countless fragments. Seritsu had poured his heart and soul into that kettle.

Instead of despair, Seritsu felt a strange calm. His grandmother's spirit whispered to him to remember the ancient art of Kintsugi—the golden repair—which was a philosophy beyond just being a technique. Brokenness was not the end, but a chance for transformation. Seritsu gathered the shards and mixed powdered gold with lacquer. With the steady hands of a surgeon, he pieced the kettle back together, tracing its fractures with shimmering lines of gold. The tea kettle emerged with radiant veins of resilience, symbols of hope and inspiration.

Word spread about Seritsu's Kintsugi bowls. Drawn by the beauty of imperfection, many arrived at the humble studio at the foothills of the towering mountains. They marveled at the golden seams—the very cracks that had once signified loss now celebrated resilience. Each ceramic piece proudly, yet humbly, displayed its unique character.

One day, an exhausted traveler named Yumi was passing through the village and stumbled upon Seritsu's humble studio. She was a broken spirit, her heart having weathered relentless storms. Seritsu offered her tea and invited her to take her time and relax in his studio. The young traveler stared at the Kintsugi pieces, tears welling in her eyes. "Tell me about these pieces," she whispered, "I want to know why I resonate with them."

Seritsu smiled. "Because they teach us that brokenness becomes beautiful. The cracks are part of our journey. Life shatters us, but we can mend. We become more beautiful and valuable precisely because of our golden scars."

Yumi chose a Kintsugi bowl—a vessel for her tears, laughter, and newfound hope. She poured tea from it, feeling the warmth of generations who had embraced their brokenness. Brokenness becomes art, and golden threads represent healing. The Kintsugi bowls stand as silent witnesses to resilience, inviting all who behold them to honor their own fractures. And that is why Kintsugi bowls are so perfectly imperfect: They remind us that our wounds make us unique and symbolize our courage to heal.

Many people work so hard to hide their imperfections and fear so greatly that others will see their wounds and flaws, yet these flaws are what make us interesting, beautiful, and unique. It's our vulnerabilities that build trusting bonds with others. No trust, no vulnerability; no vulnerability, no trust. A perfect person does not exist, never has, and never will; neither "you nor I will be the first," as Brian Johnson of Heroic likes to say. Embrace your imperfections, for they are what make you uniquely beautiful and interesting. They are not flaws, but unique features that set you apart and make you special.

I adapted this story because we all have wounds, scars, and cracks from our journeys. These don't make us less valuable; they make us more interesting and relatable. When you mend your fractures and cracks with golden lacquer threads, you radiate uniquely. No Kintsugi bowl is the same. Each one is uniquely different and beautiful as it is. Like your brain mapping and fingerprints, your unique story makes you more interesting to you and others. Celebrate your perfect imperfections instead of aiming for unattainable and less interesting perfection. Your unique story is a treasure, a celebration of your individuality and worth.

# Chapter 8

# Sixteen Types and Idiosyncratic Selves

Isabel Briggs Myers and her mother, Katherine Cook Briggs, became highly interested in Carl Jung's psychological types. As they studied these archetypes and individuals in their research lab, they began to discern four key dimensions of differences that led to them developing the Myers-Briggs Type Indicator (MBTI) for personality assessment in 1943.[20]

The four dimensions are:

- E versus I: Extrovert versus Introvert—this is how people primarily gain their emotional energy
    - extroverts gain energy by being with people
    - introverts gain energy by being alone
- S versus N: Sensing versus Intuitive—this is how people primarily gather and perceive information
    - sensing people gather information through their five senses and via facts and data
    - intuitive people gather information based on their gut feelings and impressions of patterns and possibilities
    - note that Meyers and Briggs chose an N for Intuitive because the "I" was already taken for Introvert

- F versus T: Feeling versus Thinking—this is how people primarily make decisions and use their judgment
  - feeling people consider their emotions and how others will feel when making decisions
  - thinking people use logic and facts to make decisions
- J versus P: Judging versus Perceiving—this is how people primarily orient themselves to time and change
  - judging people tend to stick with their decisions and work within deadlines
  - perceiving individuals adapt to possibilities in the moment and adapt to new information as it arises

The four pairs or dichotomies in the MBTI system result in 16 types of personalities that generally describe how individuals of those types tend to show up in the world. Each personality type comes together per how the four letters combine, representing a generalized pattern of behavior that falls on a continuum which may change over time due to factors such as significant life events, intentions to change, or misuse of drugs or alcohol. The higher the score on a particular trait, the more consistent that individual may be in displaying the associated behaviors.

Each type and its associated qualities have unique strengths and challenges; there is no "best type." Moreover, you will display your personality type uniquely from others who received the same result on their assessment because core human preferences still appear in idiosyncratic ways between individuals with identical MBTI types. The MBTI has been refined over time through various validation and reliability studies worldwide.[21] The traits and types are considered to be valid and reliable for people across different countries and cultures.

After reading the description of their results, many people might exclaim, "Wow, that describes me! I really do that." The clarity that can come from reading about themselves helps people understand how they show up, their patterns and tendencies, and how others perceive them. These descriptions can also show people where they might struggle or where others struggle to work with them.

## Types Are Not the Whole Story

Your personality, tendencies, and patterns are not the whole story of your life. A personality inventory or assessment can give you a solid direction in understanding who you are and how you appear in various contexts, and each of the sixteen personality types is on a continuum to give you a sense of where you currently fall on the spectrum of behavior preferences. However, a preference does not mean that you will behave a specific way every time. Significant life events, the use of drugs or alcohol, external circumstances, specific people, or conscious efforts to change a preference can influence how a person shows up. Lack of sleep, insufficient nourishment, illness, injury, and mental distress can also influence how someone shows up and can affect their results on the MBTI if any of those factors are at play during the time of the assessment.

Any assessment is just a snapshot in time, and it's important to consider the context when interpreting results. Personalities can be fairly stable over time, as going entirely against your patterns, preferences, and tendencies takes more energy. Allow the assessments to inform you about your preferences and tendencies thus far. Use your favorite attributes to help you formulate your Choice Identities in the functions of self, role, work or school, and relationships.

# Chapter 9

# Sociocultural Identities

Some sociocultural identities may be visible, and others may be less noticeable. Other people may generalize who you are by noticing your physical characteristics, such as your age or generation, physical abilities or differences, or your race and ethnicity. Inherited, learned, acquired, and chosen behaviors influence how people identify socioculturally. Depending on a person's stage of development, some sociocultural identities are more developed and outwardly expressed than others.

Dr. Pamela Hays examines the range of sociocultural identities in the ADDRESSING model. She notes how each relates to power differentials between groups, impacting the ways in which one sees oneself.[22] The model is an acronym for ten sociocultural identities, all of which are common to humans across the planet, although specific power differences may vary among countries. The term "power structure" refers to the distribution of power among different groups in a society, which is often influenced by sociocultural identities. In these examples, the power structure is specific to the overall culture in the United States.

The ten sociocultural characteristics of the ADDRESSING model are:

- A: age and generational influences
    - adults have more power than children, adolescents, or elders

- D: developmental disability, congenital or at birth
- individuals and groups with disabilities have less power than able-bodied people
- D: disability acquired later in life
  - individuals and groups who acquire disabilities later in life through causes such as stroke, disease, or injury have less power than able-bodied people
- R: religion and spiritual identity
  - Christians have more power than other religious or spiritual groups
- E: ethnicity or race identity
  - Caucasian people have more power than Black, Indigenous, and People of Color (BIPOC)
- S: socioeconomic status
  - middle-class people have greater access to resources than people of lower status because of occupation, education, income, and location, such as urban versus rural
- S: sexual identity
  - heterosexual people have more power status than those in LBGTQ+ communities
- I: Indigenous heritage
  - non-native individuals have more power than native or First Nations people
- N: national origin
  - US-born individuals have more power than immigrants, refugees, international students, or expatriates from non-English-speaking nations
- G: gender
  - men have more power than women or transgender and intersex people

By examining and considering these ten identities or sociocultural characteristics, individuals can explore how each identity reflects specific values or virtuous qualities. How you define yourself may limit what you think is possible for you. By carefully considering each identity type, you can discern how each of them has informed you about how you see yourself, what you believe is possible and not possible for someone with that identity, and how you can leverage the positive qualities of that identity and de-emphasize the disadvantages. Be authentic, as there is no need to buy into a belief that may not be true for you.

Are the beliefs that encompass specific identities serving you or limiting you? Which ones feel most relevant to how you think about yourself? Which ones have you taken for granted? Are the ones you take for granted related to you having more or less power as compared to the dominant group? This introspective exercise can lead to a deeper understanding of your own sociocultural identities and their influence on your life.

If you're an athlete, you may take for granted what your body can perform for you, day in and day out. Athletes and parents who are in an upper-class or middle-class socioeconomic status may take for granted the resources that are available to travel to meets and having access to uniforms, equipment, fields, and coaches that others do not.

Do your beliefs and choices enhance or diminish any of your identities? Which characteristics can you change or further develop? As you clarify your identities, keep your sociocultural attributes in mind. The next step will be to determine if your goals, values, habits, and actions align with who you are and want to become. This process of self-discovery and expanded awareness can lead to greater personal growth and a more fulfilling life.

Select the salient and most resonant values and attributes for your Choice Identities. This exercise can also open you up to learning about others' most salient sociocultural identities, especially those that are different from yours. Understanding the unique sociocultural identities of your teammates, coaches, other athletes, TAT members, or those of other parents can help strengthen the system and help you appreciate how these characteristics impact how you perceive yourself and others. Openness and curiosity about people who are different from you, as opposed to fear and distrust, allow differences to be strengths.

# Chapter 10

# Saboteurs

Carl Jung's work has had a transcendent impact on not only psychology but also on the arts, literature, philosophy, and spirituality. For example, Jung's archetypes influenced Joseph Campbell's work on The Hero's Journey, which shows up in many modern-day films and storytelling frameworks. In philosophy, Jung's ideas on individuation inspired the personal growth and self-actualization fields. Finally, Jung's work with dreams and their symbols can be seen in modern-day mysticism. His psychological types laid the groundwork for the MBTI, and in the 1920s he was the first to introduce the shadow, or hidden, aspects of personalities. He believed that accepting and integrating the shadow parts of one's personality is crucial for greater personal growth and self-awareness, thereby understanding and mastering oneself.[23] Jung's ideas influenced transpersonal, humanistic, and spiritual psychologies, all of which play a role in my own eclectic theoretical orientation.

The field of psychology has long recognized that humans have a darker or shadow side of their personalities. It is important to explore and appreciate the shadow sides of you that need to be worked on, as this is vital to succeeding on your self-mastery and confidence ownership journey and understanding yourself more deeply. Learning more about your Saboteurs is a profound place to start. Throughout your journey, recognize that you naturally have strength, gifts, and talents to offer while also recognizing that you are imperfect and have things to work on. Shunryu Suzuki, a monk who brought Zen Buddhism to the United States, said, "Each of you is perfect the way you are ... and you can use a little improvement."

Understanding where we need improvement and what is just our Saboteurs acting out of good intent is important. The reptilian part of our brain is primed to be alert to threats, whether they're real or not. To survive, humans need to anticipate danger and protect themselves by reacting quickly to avoid being harmed by physical and/or emotional threats. Like parts in the IFS model, Saboteurs are internal subpersonalities with good intentions. They react to stress and feelings of being overwhelmed in immature, unhealthy, or dysfunctional manners, but their intentions are always positive. By understanding the intents of the Saboteurs and the associated triggers that instigate an overreaction in present-day circumstances and events, we can take a pause, thank the Saboteur for the warning, and then lead from Self. The Self has the ability to talk for the part instead of the part taking over under stress and reacting with a more extreme and immature POV. Moving forward, I will use the terms "Saboteurs" and "parts" interchangeably.

Shirzad Chamine, a Stanford University business professor, created the Positive Intelligence model and the Positive Intelligence Quotient (PQ) and developed an assessment identifying ten Saboteur types that may usurp success or progress.[24] Chamine classified nine of the Saboteurs by their styles and motivations, with the tenth one being called the Master Saboteur or the Judge. The goal of Saboteurs is to protect the person from hardships, but as their name implies, Saboteurs often cause more problems than they solve.

Chamine and I do differ in how we work with the Saboteurs: He uses his model of change, whereas I pair the Saboteurs Assessment (found in

Appendix B) with the IFS approach, which allows individuals to improve the relationships between the Leader-Self and Saboteurs (parts). Clients often become curious about and get to know the positive intentions of parts non-judgmentally and with openness. As their therapist and mental performance coach, I guide the client to focus on their more prominent Saboteurs or parts that take over in reaction to experiencing stress and difficulties or overwhelming people, situations, or circumstances. I have selected a somewhat arbitrary score of 6.5 or higher as the demarcation to ask permission for the client to look more deeply at how their Saboteurs are affecting them. I selected this score because it could indicate that these Saboteurs show up more often or more strongly than other ones. Not surprisingly, in my work with athletes, many of my clients score high in the Hyper-Achiever category as being one of their top three Saboteurs.

Chamine described the types of Saboteurs by including their characteristics, thoughts, feelings, justification lies, their impacts on self and others, and original survival functions. Each type of Saboteur is categorized into one of three styles: assert, earn, or avoid, and one of three motivations: independence, acceptance, and security. For instance, the Controller Saboteur has the "assert" style and is motivated by a need for independence. Under stress, controllers tend to be aggressive or confrontational to maintain that independence and not be controlled by others. Whereas the Pleaser has an earn style that is motivated by the need for acceptance. The Pleaser does not feel like they inherently deserve to be accepted so they go about earning acceptance from others to elude their fears of rejection.

## The Ten Types of Saboteurs

Let's meet the types of Saboteurs, as described by Chamine, who may be operating behind the scenes of your behavior patterns unbeknownst to you. By bringing them into the light and pulling back the curtain, we can be more intentional about responding to challenging situations rather than one of your Saboteurs (parts) taking over and, perhaps, making things worse.

### Controller (assert style, independence motivation)

The Controller aims to assert their independence. This particular Saboteur understandably tends to be common among athletes, not to mention parents, coaches, and administrators. Athletes aim to gain as much control of themselves and others as possible while they master skills, tactics, strategies, decisions, and execution while their opponents try to do the same. Sports are dynamic and often require speed and accuracy of execution. The winners tend to be the most consistent, accurate, and timely in their execution during the competition, over the season, and in high-pressure tournament or championship situations.

The Controller has "take charge" energy that often stems from anxiety and the fear of being controlled by others or a fear of chaotic surroundings. This Saboteur can be gruff, intimidating, impatient, and even angry when things are not going their way. This part pushes other people, is willful, confrontational, and focused on winning. Believing that things will not get done, occur too slowly, or will not turn out well, the Saboteur takes over and bosses people around. Other people often resent the Controller's behavior as it comes across as insensitive, task-oriented, critical, and confrontational.

The Controller does not want to be controlled by others or by external circumstances, and paradoxically, others do not want to be controlled by the Controller! With an underlying fear of being hurt, rejected, or betrayed, it takes control to avoid feeling bad. The original survival function may be related to when a child must grow up quickly in a chaotic environment. Parents or caregivers may have neglected the child, and so the child, in their limited way, tried to handle situations when adults should have been the ones to step in. The Controller is trying its best, but it's ineffective in how it interacts with others, leaving it feeling exhausted, defeated, alone, scared, or anxious.

## Hyper-Achiever (assert style, acceptance motivation)

The Hyper-Achiever tends to also be prevalent among athletes. Anyone willing to push through physical pain with tired and sore muscles, face defeat, assert themselves against opponents, and then do it all over again likely has a need for acceptance and validation that drives them to compete and achieve. The ability to focus (or in this case, to hyper-focus) on external success such as gaining accolades, validation from others, trophies, money, fame, or popularity can have its benefits and rewards in the short run. However, the long-term consequences tend to include unsustainable workaholism, chronic injury, a potential for burnout, and a cost to relationships. The Hyper-Achiever is only satisfied with itself if it performs well, has good manners, obeys the rules, and looks good. These conditions are required for self-acceptance and self-love. Unconditionally loving oneself and experiencing love from others does not feel like an option for the Hyper-Achiever.

The Hyper-Achiever part is highly image- and status-conscious, so it molds its responses and those of others to present the perfect picture of what it thinks others would admire. This part's self-worth comes from what others think of it rather than their own feelings. They feel good when they succeed and produce results, and others admire them. Of course, these feelings tend to be short-lived until the next achievement. This Saboteur tends to keep others at a safe distance to hide imperfections and not be distracted by emotions or feelings that would keep them from succeeding. This tendency also keeps the Hyper-Achiever part from experiencing deeper emotions and a sense of self that may be vulnerable. The Hyper-Achiever has forgotten the Human-First approach, which includes experiencing vulnerability to build trusting relationships and a universal human experience.

## Restless (assert style, security motivation)

The Restless part is in constant search of the next best thing. The attitude is that there is more incredible excitement elsewhere, so it needs to keep moving and asserting itself to try to find it. The Restless part tends to bounce from thing to thing, easily distracted by more interesting shiny objects. Staying busy keeps the Restless part from finding peace or contentment with what is happening now. Paradoxically, it's seeking security. Impatience, FOMO (fear of missing out), and the fear of feeling discontent or not living a whole life are some of the thoughts and feelings of the Restless part.

Other people experience a person's Restless part as frenetic, chaotic, anxious, and superficial. Being present with unpleasant, anxious, or painful emotions drives the Restless part to keep moving in search of security. Many Restless parts feel exhausted and empty, even though it works hard to keep the Self from experiencing loneliness. The Restless part may have come into existence because the person wasn't adequately nurtured by their parents in childhood or other painful experiences that the Restless part thinks may overwhelm the internal system.

## Stickler (earn style, independence motivation)

The Stickler part aims to earn independence by being overly organized and perfectionistic, often being highly critical of its own performance and that of others. It tends to be sensitive to criticism often because it's been judgmental and critical of itself. It does not need anyone else to point out their flaws. The Stickler invests an incredible amount of extra work to ensure that things get done with the highest standards. The Stickler part often finds itself doing extra work because it believes others don't know what they are doing or are just sloppy and lazy.

Interactions with others tend to err on using criticism, irritability, resentment, sarcasm, and opinions to make others conform to their ideal standards, which tend to be black or white, right or wrong, with little room for anything in between. The Stickler part rarely seems pleased with others' work and is very demanding of itself. Aiming to be perfect can allay others' criticism. This form of protection gives a form of temporary self-satisfaction. This part may have formed during one's childhood in response to trying to earn acceptance and attention from demanding and emotionally unavailable parents. Acting like an unreproachable, perfect kid may have made the Stickler feel protected from criticism or rejection and kept the Self from feeling unlovable and abandoned.

## Pleaser (earn style, acceptance motivation)

The Pleaser part aims to earn acceptance by helping, flattering, and rescuing others, all at the cost of their own needs. Being liked, reassured, and accepted, and receiving affection are all crucial needs of the Pleaser part; however, it has indirect methods and seemingly altruistic ways that leave people feeling manipulated to reciprocate care. The Pleaser part's methods are passive-aggressive, while the behaviors come across as being selfless and generous in putting other people's needs first and being a good person serving others. However, these acts are performative in that the Pleaser part seeks acceptance and attention, leaving the person feeling drained, resentful, and burned out when its emotional needs are unmet.

Other people may get frustrated with a Pleaser part who does not ask for or accept help. The Pleaser part expects others to read its mind and meet its needs but will not explicitly say what its needs are for fear of appearing selfish or demanding, having learned to believe that love and attention are earned by giving it away and putting others' needs before its own. Expecting love to be reciprocated equivalently without asking for it leaves the Pleaser part feeling resentful and other people feeling confused by the passive-aggressive resentment that is enacted but not discussed.

## Hypervigilant (earn style, security motivation)

The Hypervigilant part aims to earn security by over-indexing concerns about dangers, threats, fears, and what could potentially go wrong. The core belief of the Hypervigilant part is that life is full of hazards, so it is overly alert and sensitive to its environment because a threat to safety and security might be life-threatening or overwhelmingly painful. It tries to prevent bad things from happening by being skeptical, cynical, and highly anxious.

How other people experience the Hypervigilant part is that it's draining to be around. Others may notice that a great deal of energy gets wasted on worrying over threats that never turn into anything, and they may start tuning out the Hypervigilant part. Mark Twain is known for having said, "I've had a lot of troubles in my life, most of which never happened." The Hypervigilant part may have experienced a lack of reliable, predictable safety and security in their parental figures, and/or life-threatening events. It does its best to try to predict and warn others, but hypervigilance is problematic when that part cannot take a break and relax.

## Avoider (avoid style, independence motivation)

The Avoider part aims to avoid independence by focusing on positive, pleasant, and pleasurable experiences at the cost of facing reality. It is afraid of losing connection with others by being in conflict with them or hurting others' feelings. The Avoider part often says yes to things it doesn't want just to maintain connection. This part is also afraid that the task, conflict, or situation will be too unpleasant, so it procrastinates to keep things friendly, balanced, and peaceful.

The Avoider part may view itself as being flexible and a peacemaker. However, other people tend to mistrust the Avoider part because it withholds information, using passive-aggressive behavior instead of dealing with conflict and challenges head-on. The Avoider may have learned this approach from being raised in a family with high conflict and tension and learned that a peacemaker should not add any stress or negativity. Conversely, the Avoider part may have emerged from a happy childhood where difficult emotions were not dealt with or faced. Either way, the child did not learn the ability to handle challenges with resiliency so it would prefer to avoid them altogether.

## Victim (avoid style, acceptance motivation)

The Victim part aims to avoid acceptance because it fears something is wildly wrong with them. The Victim part reacts with extreme emotions when it feels criticized, misunderstood, or overly challenged. Having a core belief that something is wrong with it, the Victim part seeks inklings of affection and attention from those who may not otherwise pay them much heed. The Victim part broods in the hopes that someone will comfort them by saying it's not their fault and that they are an okay and acceptable person. The part has a disposition of feeling that bad things always happen to them, that they must be uniquely flawed or disadvantaged, and that someone should rescue them from their situation.

Unfortunately, the approach of envy, negativity, and feeling sorry for oneself tends to backfire by pushing people away. Other people view the part as dramatic, sullen, and withdrawing to gain attention, love, validation, or affection. To others, the Victim part can appear as wanting to be a martyr. Other people may feel guilty that they are not able to help the Victim feel better as the brooding, sadness, and pain seem unconquerable. The Victim part likely emerged from having learned that dramatic reactions are the only way to gain acceptance and be seen or heard.

## Hyper-Rational (avoid style, security motivation)

The Hyper-Rational part aims to avoid feeling insecure by rationalizing, analyzing, and intellectualizing the "whys" of life. Rather than engaging in the feelings and emotions of circumstances, people, and events, the Hyper-Rational part observes from a distance, often coming across as intellectually superior and arrogant. By focusing on and mastering knowledge, facts, information, and data, the Hyper-Rational part feels worthy and competent, whereas needs and emotions are distractions from this higher level of being.

Other people may feel that they're not being valued and cared for while interacting with the Hyper-Rational part, as work and intellectual pursuits are its priorities. The Hyper-Rational part likely arose from the person having had emotionally tumultuous childhood experiences and experiencing chaotic environments. Survival was sought through developing a neat, orderly, predictable mind space. The Hyper-Rational part gained praise, attention, and admiration by showing up as the intellectually superior person in the room. However, this stance could also backfire with the part being perceived as cold, distant, and intimidating.

## Master Saboteur

Like the Inner Critic in the IFS model, the Master Saboteur (also known as the Judge) internally pushes you to improve and succeed by using blame, fear, anxiety, judgment, guilt, shame, and badgering tactics. These tactics can manifest in various ways, such as self-criticism, fear of failure, or a constant feeling of not being good enough. The Judge works with the other more prominent Saboteurs in your internal system in the hopes of helping you succeed, but unfortunately, this approach often leaves a person feeling full of doubt and self-blame and lacking trust in the Leader-Self. The Judge's Original Survival Function is to notice, exaggerate, and react quickly to negativity or threats in the environment to survive and keep its person safe. Evolution has honed the skills of the Judge to detect the slightest indicators of threat in the environment and then send out its best soldier (another Saboteur or more) to protect the system. Unfortunately, the Judge can misjudge and overreact to the threat as being more significant than it actually is. Often it is not a genuine danger but rather an unpleasant person, situation, or circumstance whereby the Judge has misjudged reality.

## Shadow Sides: Now What?

Now that you have a high-level overview of each of the Saboteurs or the shadow sides, parts, or subpersonalities of the Self, we can begin to work on developing a relationship with the predominant parts that blend or take over more often, and on how to meet their needs. The IFS process helps Saboteurs identify how to use their energy differently and for the greater good of a person's internal harmony. External familial, friend, partner, or team relationships often improve when each role in the system works internally to help their Saboteurs before lashing out and blaming others. As each individual develops trust in their own Leader-Self, both the internal and external systems harmonize.

Most people don't like their Saboteurs or parts, and their initial reaction is to reject them, as the Saboteurs have been destructive and can seem so negative. Sometimes, the parts come across so strongly that one might wonder, "Is this just who I am?" These are parts of you, not the whole of you. These parts have good intentions but have a wonky approach because they emerged at younger ages in response to trauma, hurt, disappointment, and perceived failure. At the time, there was likely not an adult available to effectively help you manage your reaction to difficult situations, so your internal system took over. The parts aim to be helpful and protect the system, but the part or protector has limited, immature skills and did the best it could with the development it had at the time.

The Leader-Self was still developing in childhood, so it had not acquired the skills to step in and handle tough situations from a higher point of view. To gain harmony and relationship with the parts, the Leader-Self must establish a trusting, curious, and open relationship through inner conversation with each part to help it feel understood and appreciated for its efforts. Once trust is established between the Self and the Saboteur part and the part witnesses the Leader-Self fulfilling its role effectively, the part can relax and decide to use its energy differently. Often, the Saboteurs then become the best cheerleaders in supporting the internal family system.

You may have begun to see how the internal family system gets projected outward within a team environment or in your external family, as similar dynamics may erupt with the intent of self-protection but may have poor results and a lousy impact. When teammates, coaches, and parents talk from the Self and for their parts, the outcomes of the conversation have a much greater chance of success as compared with when part-to-part communication is occurring. Under threat and fear, the parts can come out to protect the person, but because it's immature and has fewer skillful means, it often causes more harm than good.

Even if someone else is talking from a part and being ineffective, when you're in your Self-energy and speaking from your Leader-Self, you can positively impact the conversation and relationship by influencing a more effective conversation. Speaking from the Leader-Self is a form of self-mastery by remaining in control of your internal state.

Working with your Saboteur parts empowers you to avoid sabotaging your goals or relationships when your parts get scared, threatened, or overwhelmed. Recognizing your Saboteurs will also help you express compassion for yourself and others and not take other people's destructive behaviors so personally. You can remain connected when someone else speaks from their part instead of for their part. By understanding your character strengths and shadow parts, your goals can be pursued using your strengths and not be thwarted by your Saboteurs. Pursue your most important goals with your strongest character attributes, winning at both self-mastery and goal achievement.

## How to Review the Saboteurs Assessment

Complete the free Saboteurs Assessment online (see the references section in the appendix), then review the descriptions of your Saboteurs with the top three scores. Typically, the higher the score (6.5 or above), the more the descriptions, thoughts, and feelings tend to resonate with you. Underline, circle, star, or highlight the aspects of your Saboteur profiles that most reflect your experience of you. With my clients, we discuss the descriptions and characteristics in depth.

This awareness-building and deep dive exercise into who you are can help you understand your basic identities, which are the building blocks to your Human-First identity, Choice Identities, and the foundation of the confident performer model. This model is a framework for personal development and performance enhancement, particularly in sports or high-performance contexts. These foundational activities are the path to developing solid confidence in various circumstances in your life, including sports, work, and relationships.

By normalizing your Saboteurs and understanding their positive intent but not-so-great behaviors, I encourage you to have compassion for yourself and others. A foundational principle in mental health is remembering that you are not alone in your human experiences. By normalizing and accepting that the Saboteur or part is trying to protect you, you can begin to acknowledge and appreciate its efforts while helping it recognize that it is ineffective at its job and is exhausting the system. Once it learns to trust the Leader-Self, the part might consider finding another more productive way to help the internal system.

## For You, Not to You

Your Leader-Self has a belief that things happen for you and not to you, which helps you maintain consistent peace of mind. This foundational belief helps harmonize the Saboteurs instead of triggering them into becoming reactive. The Leader-Self can help a Saboteur shift from anger, hurt, or sadness to having acceptance, learning a lesson, or feeling that something even better is around the corner. Think of a time when your victim Saboteur got activated or when something unfortunate or disappointing happened to you. In this case, we are not talking about trauma with a big T. When you look back, are there lessons you gleaned from the experience? What did you learn about yourself or others that is meaningful? When the situation is reframed as happening for you to understand, can you see a new path forward that may be a better road for you? How would you emotionally recover in a more holistic way by considering that something happened for you instead of to you? As in the drama triangle, sometimes you are a victim of a crime or bad behavior done to you by others or are caught in the crosshairs of bad timing where the situation is entirely out of your hands. But if we glean the lessons learned, we can often see the value of what happened, since we cannot change that it happened.

# CHAPTER 11

# Goals and Intentions

During my athletic career, I had the fantastic opportunity to play collegiately and on the global stage with some of the best athletes in the world in my sport of field hockey. In college, my coaches were three-time Olympian Beth Beglin and two-time Olympian goalkeeper Patti Shea, who was also my Olympic teammate. The University of Iowa and 1988 Olympic assistant coach, Michele "Mad-Dog" Madison, recruited me to join the defending university national championship team. Dr. Judith Davidson, the head coach when I was a freshman, was the only coach of a women's team at Iowa who won a national championship and built a top program in a state that didn't even sponsor the sport of field hockey. The standards at Iowa were and remain high today. Olympians were developing future Olympians and I wanted to be one of the greats, inspired by Iowa's legacy. I started to believe that I could be one of the best goalies in the country and become an Olympian.

One day in the locker room, I distinctly remember looking up to the border between the top of the wall and the ceiling and seeing the photos posted of every All-American athlete who had played for Iowa since the start of the varsity field hockey program. Having been recruited into the reigning national championship team, I felt pressure as a freshman on the inside that I didn't show on the outside. The remit was clear from Coach Davidson: I would train under and learn from the All-America, senior and defending national champion goalkeeper Karen Napolitano. Karen was a fantastic goalie and was touted to go onto the national team. Unfortunately, she injured her knee during pre-season, leaving the door open for me to start as a goalkeeper for the defending national championship team.

I was terrified but pretended not to be. I somehow acquired mononucleosis during pre-season and had to sit out the first five games of the season while one of our star athletes and former soccer player, Erin Walsh, who had never played goalie before, suited up and learned quickly how to play the position. This experience taught me that things can change rapidly, so one must always be ready for opportunities. No one expected the senior goalie to get injured and to have a first-year goalie step in to play, or for the only goalie left to get sick and have a defender, who knew how to use her feet from soccer, step in to play goalie for a top Division I program while having never played the position.

If you have standards of excellence and prepare yourself to the utmost of your ability, you will be more ready to step in than if your preparation had been lackluster. Consider your sources of inspiration, your role models and heroes, learn from what they do best, and adopt their greatest virtues and habits. My inspirational sources spurred me and the Iowa team on to four final four appearances, and multiple accolades and recognitions. You will hopefully discover that the same virtues you admire in the people who inspire you are already present within you.

## Three Big WIGs

Goals provide the motivation, direction, and inspiration for us to act, make choices, and shape life experiences. They affect who you meet and with whom you work. They are the gifts and experiences life gives you and that you can earn. Goals can shape who you become. In their book, *The 4*

*Disciplines of Execution*, Chris McChesney, Sean Covey, and Jim Huling talk about Wildly Important Goals (WIGs), and in the book, *Built to Last*, Jim Collins and Jerry Porras discuss Big, Hairy, Audacious Goals (BHAGs) for leaders and organizations.[25] [26] Regardless of what you call them, having clear intentions or goals is vital to providing you with the direction, focus, motivation, and inspiration to act, especially when you don't feel like it.

Two of the WIGs or BHAGs that ultimately shaped my life, I set at an early age. The first one was to be an Olympian; I set that goal at age six after watching Nadia Comaneci score perfect 10s in the 1976 Olympic gymnastics. The second one was to be a psychologist; I set that goal at age 11 when I would mimic my dad, who was a psychiatrist. I would conduct "talk sessions" with my friends to help them with their boy or girl problems or help another six-grader with the challenges they were struggling with. Now, I find myself at the intersection of supporting high-performance individuals, teams, and leaders who I help to own their confidence while becoming the better to best version of themselves in all arenas.

What are your WIGs or BHAGs? What will challenge you? What feels entirely out of reach but not out of sight? What will require the best of you consistently, day after day, in order to reach? Why do you want to achieve it? What will it say about you? What do you want to learn about yourself and others by really going for it? These goals should be challenging, but not impossible. They may beat you up, spit you out, disappoint you, and make you feel like a failure even though you're not, but you will learn more about what to do more of and what needs work when finding out who you are and what you can achieve. Setting something easily achievable is not really a goal; it's something that you can already do. Make it challenging.

When I worked with a team of mental conditioning coaches at the world-renowned sports school IMG Academy, most of them did not want goal setting to be a part of the curriculum. As the head of the department, I was incredulous. For me, goal setting was the foundation of mental performance. For decades, I taught four core mental skills: goal-setting, breathing, self-talk and body language, and mental rehearsal. To me, no goal setting meant no direction, motivation, inspiration, or reason to act. I learned that people from generations younger than mine were afraid to set goals because of fear of failure if they did not reach them. Well, that did not jive with me. Goals make life more interesting and tie into your Choice Identities by guiding who you need to become in order to reach your most important goals. Attributes such as discipline, focus, hard work ethic, coachability, adaptability, growth mindset, resilience, persistence and perseverance are all attributes that you will likely need on your goal-pursuing adventure. What other attributes and values aligned with behavior will you need to consistently show up as your best self to achieve your goals?

To achieve my Olympic Dream, I had to consistently show up to practice and training with the willingness to work hard, stay focused, listen and act on coaching and feedback, encourage and correct my teammates, and encourage and correct myself for countless hours over the span of 21 years. Each time I got cut from a tour or tournament team (totaling 13 times), I had to return to the drawing board to improve my accuracy, speed, power, consistency, and confidence. Today, I also consider what I need to do less of. I assessed what I needed to adjust most to make the team at the following selection. I had to think, act, and feel like an Olympian to become one, even when others had their doubts.

Using a straightforward method of goal setting, write down at least three WIGs for yourself. They might be near-term, in the next 3–12 months, or far away, such as 5, 10, or 20 years from now. You can use the prompts below if you find them helpful. You may have heard of SMART goals, an acronym for specific, measurable, achievable, realistic, and timely, and likewise, your goals should be focused on specificity, objectivity, possibility, timeliness, and positivity. Another scientifically validated goal-setting formula is Dr. Gabriele Oettingen's WOOP model, an acronym for wish, outcome, obstacles, and plan.[27]

1.  Wish: What are your highest priority goals that are specific and meaningful?

2.  Outcome: Imagine the life-changing result of achieving it. How will it feel? What will it sound like and look like? How will you know you achieved it?

3.  Obstacles: Consider the challenges you may face. What might you have to go around, over, under, or through to keep making progress toward your goal(s)? Some of these challenges may include:

    a.  Fear: Can I even do it? Will it be too hard? How much time, effort, and money will it take? What if I don't achieve it; what will that say about me? Will people judge or criticize me for having this goal, and what if I fail?

    b.  Laziness: Saying to yourself "I don't feel like it" (the five most goal-sabotaging words).

3.  Plan: Use performance goals, process goals, and algorithms such as if-then strategies to overcome the obstacles to break down the bigger goal into more manageable chunks by thinking of them as stepping stones or rungs on a ladder as you progress.

    a.  Plan for setbacks, disappointments, and missteps and how you will recover and bounce back from them.

    b.  Include your support system to ask for help, encouragement, and accountability.

Goals are meant to be out of reach and challenging but ultimately achievable, even if they are extremely difficult. Turn impossible into "I'm possible." If you didn't censor, limit, or argue against yourself, what WIGs or BHAGs would you set for yourself? Mark Divine, author of *Unbeatable Mind*, says we can achieve 20 times what we think we can achieve.[28] Remembering the four primary domains of life: Leader-Self, work or school, role (parent, athlete, coach, or TAT), and relationships, keep answering the questions below by filling in the blanks until you get a list of goals, intentions, or targets that excite you about shaping a fantastic life.

- Achieve _____ by the year or date _____. Why?
- Be a(n) _____ by the year or date _____. Why?
- Be known for _____ by the year or date _____. Why?

## Algorithms to Support Your WIGs

Goal setting and maintaining intentions help focus the mind on what outcomes you want. However, just because you set a goal, create clear and specific plans, and work hard does not always mean you will achieve your objective. Algorithms are one of the best planning tools for any performer to use in moving toward their goals and responding effectively to mistakes when things don't go as planned. Military and business leaders call it contingency planning. "If this, then that" statements can help leaders and confident performers think through the possibilities of what can or might happen. They also can be used as pre-commitments so decision fatigue is reduced. By thinking through possible solutions and making pre-commitments, the confident performer can respond quickly and efficiently to changing or unexpected situations since things do not always go to plan. We must prepare for the unexpected while we simultaneously prepare for amazing.

Examples of pre-commitments might include:

- If it's 10 p.m., then I am preparing for bed.
- If it's MWF at 4 p.m., I am lifting with my teammate at the school gym.

- If it's 15 minutes before practice, I am setting my practice goals and mindset to have a productive practice.

Examples of algorithms to prepare for the unexpected:

- If we arrive late to a game due to traffic, we will execute our shortened warm-up to still be ready and focused by the whistle.
- If the other team is double-teaming me, I will pass earlier and keep my game simple.
- If we are down by two goals in the first 15 minutes, we will maintain composure, slow things down with short, simple plays to hold on to possession, regain momentum, and then pick our moments to attack.

Algorithms help make the complex simpler. As an example, a soccer athlete at the Air Force Academy asked me to help him to not panic when the pressure was on while he was playing. He described the scenario as knowing what he wanted to do when he trapped the ball, but then his first and second options closed and the pressure increased as two opponents closed in on him. We discussed developing "if-then" statements to make the complex situation more simple and efficient. For example, "If my first two options are unavailable, then I will pass the ball back to my teammate to maintain possession." Or "If I'm holding onto the ball too long, then I will look to two-touch the next play by fully scanning what's available before receiving the ball." Or "If I can take on the defenders to get to open space, then I will confidently take them on." The algorithm makes the decision ahead of time based on the conditions you set, allowing for more efficiency and less overthinking while performing. After the performance, look at how the algorithm worked and if anything needs refinement.

In data science, scientists use algorithms to quickly and efficiently simplify a tremendous amount of data. In high-performance sports, athletes can get caught up and distracted by overthinking. The best athletes and GOATs have simplified the game or competition; they know when to focus on specific cues to execute accurately and efficiently. This comes from countless reps, a great deal of experience with what didn't work, and learning and applying what does work. People who are experts in a field have invested years into becoming the authentic authorities they are. There are no shortcuts. However, by working smarter via implementing algorithms into your performance planning and thinking through your contingency plans, you will likely find yourself responding more effectively and reacting with less panic.

I encourage you to write up to 50 "if-then" statements to support the four identities: your Leader-Self and how you want to show up; your relationships and who you want to be, especially in situations where you find yourself feeling caught off guard; your work or school where you want to be at your best and also prepare for unexpected circumstances; and in your current role as a parent, athlete, coach, TAT member, or administrator. Recall two or three keystone algorithms before your next performance and begin testing them. Notice whether algorithms help you think and respond efficiently and optimally, allowing you to own your confidence and self-mastery. If you implement and test your algorithms, celebrate and high-five your inner self for taking action, then lather, rinse, and repeat!

## Examples of algorithms for Choice identities:

Leader-Self: If I'm' getting irritated in traffic, which causes me to be late, then I will extend my exhale, keep my body relaxed, and practice self-mastery. If it's mealtime, I will have colorful fruits and veggies, a protein source, and complex carbs like a sweet potato or wild grains. If it's before noon, then I will get my fitness in.

Work/School. If it's work or homework time, I will block off 75 minutes of deep work, turning off my phone and focusing on the task at hand. If I am leading a project or meeting, then I will listen to and ask for input before summarizing what I have heard, suggesting direction and clarifying action items and commitments prior to the next meeting.

Role: If it's game week, then I will get organized for my role and how I can contribute while remembering that I will contribute to our collective positive sporting experience.

Relationship: If it's family dinner time, then I will ask that all phones be put away so we can connect as a family and hear about how things are going. If I'm getting frustrated that something I asked to be done isn't done, I will inquire first and then use the Nonviolent Communication model (Observations, Feelings, Needs, Requests) to make a request and come to an agreement. If I hear of a good gift idea for someone I care about, I will write it down so I can remember to get it on a special occasion.

# Chapter 12

# Choice Identities and Alignment with Goals

The power of Choice Identities lies in us designing how we want to show up in the identities of Self, role, work or school, and relationships. These intentionally defined identities shape and influence our beliefs, actions, decisions, and with whom we affiliate. Identities go deeper than roles by getting to core values, attributes, and beliefs that often dictate behavior. Understanding, designing, and aligning these Choice Identities with our goals is crucial for personal growth, self-improvement, and goal attainment. Humans are complex, but you can take the best of your tendencies, patterns, and attributes to develop your Choice Identities. So let's take a look at how all the sources work together.

Our primary identity is natural intelligence; the Human First identity also known as your Self or Leader-Self. Understanding the basis of who we are gives us the best source of perspective, power, and a sense of connection. Loving-kindness is the basis of who we are; we can have a constant source of safety and belonging. The Leader-Self is naturally occurring and reflects natural intelligence or ever-present awareness without effort. According to IFS, we are born with qualities of Self-energy, referred to as the 8 Cs (compassion, curiosity, confidence, courage, calm, connectedness, clarity, and creativity). We can lead from Self-energy in any situation when we remember to tap into what's already present. Tuning in may require slowing down and taking a breath if the situation affords you the time.

Patterns and tendencies related to personality clusters are expressed in the individual's idiosyncratic personality, which is both inherited and learned. The MBTI, and other personality inventories, maps out how individuals tend to gain and recover energy (Introvert vs Extrovert), how they prefer to access information (Sensing versus Intuitive), how they tend to make decisions (Thinking versus Feeling), and how they prefer to orient to time and space (Judging versus Perceiving). Personality type assessments can help you better understand your and others' tendencies and patterns, and their differences, and determine why those differences add strength to the group, family, or team. We also know that personality types do not fully encompass and predict who a person is.

Sociocultural identities (the ADDRESSING model) are related to genetic inheritance, the time and place of their presence, and learned sociocultural experiences. Sociocultural identities can be a source of pride and strength for an individual by identifying with the strengths and values of their culture and with whom they affiliate. The identities correlate with power structures and vary from country to country and can impact how individuals view themselves and others, and how others in turn view and treat them.

Saboteurs are subpersonalities formed due to traumatic experiences, difficulties, intense emotions, and hurt. Distinguishing them as parts rather than the whole of who you are creates more space for you to respond to difficulties and challenges intentionally instead of reacting in unhelpful ways. All parts have good intentions but are often ineffective at their job and can cause unnecessary damage to oneself and often others. Recognizing triggers, fears, and reactions in the moment and pausing before responding allows you to move more easily into one of your Choice

Identities. Ask yourself, "What's the best identity for the job at hand, and which attributes will optimize the outcome?" For example, do I need to be a fierce competitor and use dominance, strength, and intense trust in myself? Or do I need to be an open, listening, good friend for my teammate who just lost an important match?

Now that you have a deeper understanding of your multiple selves and why and how those patterns and tendencies developed, you can draw on the best of you to identify your ultimate Choice Identities. Volumes of research journals, books, and articles and fields of study are dedicated to exploring human identity, personality types, sociocultural identity development, the shadow sides of personality, and how much control we have over who we are. Lay out on the table your best virtues, attributes, tendencies, patterns, and likely responses to view your options. Then, make deliberate decisions about which aspects you want to keep, accept, celebrate, accentuate, discard, reduce, or minimize. Consider who you need to become to progress and achieve your WIGs.

## GIVBA: Aligning Goals, Attributes, Behaviors, and Algorithms with Identity

With a better understanding of your sources of Self, it's time to align your attributes and behaviors with your Choice Identities. Writing down your Choice Identities is the first step. Otherwise, you're just intellectualizing or theorizing instead of practicing and mastering. Intellectualizing about change rarely leads to actual change.

Most people struggle to title or name their Choice Identities, while others feel challenged by narrowing down their key attributes and virtues. You may not need to narrow them, but a longer list will be more difficult to commit to memory and action. If you struggle to differentiate between virtue, or attribute, and behavior, you're not alone. Ask, "What would other people see you doing when you put your best attributes into action?"

Persistence may look like continually working to make a team despite repeated setbacks, disappointments, and other obstacles. Setbacks may include having an injury or being cut from the team repeatedly, and yet you still find a way toward your goal. Discipline might look like waking up day after day at 6 a.m. to meditate for 15 minutes, even when everything inside you says, "I don't feel like it." Courage might look like having a difficult conversation with someone you care about even when it seems easier to ignore the problem and move on.

Charting out a five by four table in your journal or on an index card with your daily identities, virtues, and target behavior may be helpful. See the references section of the appendix for more information on the Heroic.us app that may also be helpful. The table below is inspired by and adapted from Heroic. us, but it's not exactly the same. If you use the app, it will look different. In Heroic.us language, "Every day is Day One," so it is important every day to close the gap between where you are today and your optimal, heroic selves, knowing that some days you will do this well, and other days, you will have setbacks or slip-ups. Simply get back on track as soon as you can.

Using your journal, create a table such as the one below:

|  | S = Self | R = Role | W = Work or School | L= Love and Relationships |
|---|---|---|---|---|
| G = Goals |  |  |  |  |
| I = Identity |  |  |  |  |
| V = Virtues |  |  |  |  |
| B = Behaviors |  |  |  |  |
| A = Algorithms |  |  |  |  |

Complete the table by asking yourself the following questions:

- Goals: What are my WIGs?
  - Choose only one or two of your most important ones in each area to keep your efforts focused, as too many goals may be overwhelming.
- Identity: Who do I need to become to be the kind of person who can achieve that goal? Some examples include the:
  - healthy, confident performer
  - relentless defender
  - courageous , clear communicator-coach
  - patient, emotionally available parent
  - persistent, consistent student
  - confident leader or manager
  - listening lover
  - encouraging friend or teammate
- Virtues/Attributes: What virtues and values best reflect who I want to be and what matters to me most in order to become the identity that can reach my WIGs?
- Behaviors: What behaviors reflect the kind of person I want to be and represent the virtues and values that matter most to me?
- Algorithms: What "if-then" algorithms can I implement to help me automate my behavior?
  - Have an algorithm to counteract when you hear yourself say, "I don't feel like it." These five words are goal-sabotaging words. Confident performers may hear themselves saying those five detrimental, motivation-killing words sometimes, but they usually find a way to override them with an algorithm.

For example, If I hear myself saying "I don't feel like it," then I will count down from ten and launch into the activity I'm avoiding.

When working with teams, I will have coaches and athletes include at least two of their team values in their role identity statements. I also ask parents and coaches to include the team and organizational values in their role identity statements. Regardless of your role, you're part of a system that you're helping to win, while also winning with character.

Remember that identities, attributes, and values evolve over time. What you write today is not concrete. You and your identities will change and evolve with time. You might set a specific identity for a particular situation and how you wish to show up for those unique circumstances. Although you should not necessarily change your colors like a chameleon for every situation, you should draw on your best virtues, favorite attributes, and most effective behaviors to get the best possible outcomes in each circumstance.

Using your journal, index cards for each identity, or the Heroic.us app, you can pre-plan how you intend to show up rather than being caught off guard and not knowing how to respond. Even beginners in new situations can show up as the better to best version of themselves. They might ask questions, observe to learn, and maintain a posture of curiosity and openness. By disconnecting confidence from competence, you empower yourself to enter a new situation with zero competence but with the confidence to enact your most curious, open-to-learning characteristics.

Use your reflection practices at the end of each day to glean the learning, growth, and refinement of how aligned you were with your intentions. This process is about continuous improvement and realignment as you learn more and more about yourself and how you intend to show up. High-five yourself and celebrate when you do show up in the intended ways. When your actions fall out of alignment, find where you need some work and adjust your intentions to show up more in alignment next time. Shaming, blaming, and complaining do not help your brain learn, nor do they keep your spirits high in the Game of self-mastery, so use that energy to learn instead. Reset your sights on improvement and celebrate your progress and expanding awareness.

## Letting Go of Perfectionism (the Stickler's Primary Value)

Choice Identities are not about perfection—they are always a work in progress. By increasing our awareness and understanding of ourselves and others, we can recognize that nobody is perfect, or rather that we are all perfect the way we are, and we can all use some improvement. Perfectionism tends to get in the way of progress and performance. Both require joy and freedom to achieve the excellence you seek.

Choice Identities are the persons we want to be, especially in challenging situations. We have the freedom to define and adapt how we want to show up in our Self, role, work or school, and love and relationships, and we are not always going to get it right. It's a practice, and the practice leads to self-mastery and confidence ownership, not perfection. Besides, nobody likes a perfect person. We typically connect with others through our vulnerabilities, authenticity, and common humanity.

Let's look at the four Choice Identities more carefully, starting with the Self.

### Self-Identity

The Self is a collaborative, co-creative process between your inner being and the source from which you emanate. Depending on your religious or spiritual beliefs, you may call this source universal energy, life force, God, Brahman, Yahweh, Atman, Allah, Great Spirit, Tao, Chi, Qi, prana, Shakti, natural intelligence, Holy Spirit, Shekhinah, Divine Intelligence, universal consciousness, or something else per your understanding of what forces brought you to life. Part of your human responsibility is to care for your mind, body, and emotions so that your spirit or inner being can fully express itself. Your Self-Identity, or Leader Self, is who you are when you are at ease, naturally present in the moment, energized, clear, calm, and confident. In this identity, all eight Cs from the IFS model are naturally present without effort.

## Role identity

In the winning systems framework, I have talked about the core four roles of the PACT (parent, athlete, coach, and TAT members) which looks at the team and the organization as a system. In this exercise, focus on creating your role identity as it relates to the PACT. Consider three to five virtues and values for your role identity, then create your targeted actions that align with goals in the PACT system.

For example:

- Goal: To encourage Eva's and my positive contribution to the common goal of having a positive experience in travel softball this season.
- Identity:
  o present and nurturing parent
- Virtues and values:
  o attentive listening
  o affectionate and warm
  o high standards
  o accountability
  o honesty
  o following through on family commitments
- Target behaviors:
  o take a 10–15 minute walk most days with dog, spouse or partner, and Eva to connect after work
  o ask open-ended questions regarding practice or school, what was fun, how you challenged yourself, and what you found most interesting or surprising

    o   give 8–20 second hugs to boost oxytocin (the brain's love and emotional closeness hormone) at least twice daily to each family member.

## Work identity

For high school and college athletes, you might identify your work identity as being a high-performing student-athlete. You might also identify your future work identity as a senior business leader, educator, engineer, teacher, nurse, zookeeper, or other profession that intrigues you. You can consider your industry, career projection, or current employment and then add the virtues and behaviors that are consistent with you at your best.

## Love and relationship identity

Love and relationship identity refers to a broad definition of love and relationships. It includes family, friends, teammates, schoolmates, teachers, coaches, and even people in your community. An example of creating targeted actions based on identifying your virtues and values is presented below.

- Goal: To make three new trustworthy friends at school this year
- Identity:
  - easy-going, humorous friend
- Virtues and values:
  - curious
  - relaxed
  - playful
  - fun
- Behaviors:
  - encourage someone today
  - offer to help someone without being asked (carry groceries, open a door, ask a new person at class to eat lunch together, offer to study math together)

o    ask open-ended questions about how someone is doing

o    smile and make eye contact

## Superpowers and Kryptonite

Heroes and heroines have superpowers, and they also have weaknesses or Kryptonite. What's the one non-negotiable behavior that makes for a better day when you do it and feels like a superpower to you? For some people, it might be getting a great night's sleep, meditating, being in nature, eating a healthy meal, or running their morning routine to feel right with themselves. The six fundamentals of a whole person/healthy performers discussed in Chapter 13 are typical superpowers for many people. For me, it's exercise: I feel much better about myself and it's harder to have a bad day when I've had a good workout, and conversely, I feel worse when I do not exercise. When I was younger and in a grouchy mood, my mom would suggest that I go for a run. It's hard to come back from a vigorous workout and feel worse, even if you may feel more tired. What is your non-negotiable for feeling good? Can you get your superpower practice in every day? The idea is that without that one thing, your superpower, you don't feel like yourself. You feel off, and those who know you best know you are off, too.

Decide on that one thing that makes your day go better, and let other people close to you know that your daily thing is non-negotiable for you to be at your best. When you have communicated this in advance, your support system can encourage you to help and will be less likely to criticize you when you need to get it done. After you've chosen your most important non-negotiable behavior and established a habit of executing it every day, choose another one that is harder for you and see what small and reasonable steps you can make consistently to make gains in the one fundamental that you are not as good about achieving. Make your reasonable steps so small that you cannot fail! Your energy, sense of self, and whole health and performance will take a turn for the better as a result.

What about the behaviors or actions that tend to make you feel bad? Feeling bad can trigger more bad feelings and behaviors. Perhaps you were put down or insulted at school or work. Did you believe the person's comments and then feel worse about yourself? Did you find yourself feeling distracted by the mean thing that someone said? You could create an "if-then" algorithm for work or school. For example, if someone insults or puts me down, I will say, "I don't understand what you mean by that." If the person cannot explain or it's made clear that they were just being mean because they were having a bad day, you don't need to take it personally or internalize the comment. If you feel bad because of having had a poor night's sleep, perhaps it happened because you were on your device too late at night and you didn't give yourself enough time to complete a project because of procrastination. Planning for avoiding or dealing with your kryptonite, which makes you feel weak and incompetent, will help you feel in control and less overwhelmed. One of the biggest kryptonite statements is "I don't feel like it!" Be sure to have a counter statement for those words, such as those encouraged by Mel Robbins in her book The 5 *Second* Rule "5-4-3-2-1 Go!"[29] Then go and do an action, no matter how small, toward the activity you are avoiding.

Give some reflection time to what makes you feel good and what makes you feel upset, hurt, angry, disappointed, and sad. By knowing these in advance, you can plan ahead of time how you can help yourself. Sometimes, acknowledging what you are feeling without trying to change the feeling is a great place to start. Celebrate and high-five your inner being for the dopamine win if you feel good after doing the thing you said you would do. Allow your feelings to be as they are if you feel sad, hurt, or angry. Simply acknowledging, instead of dismissing, your feelings can help soften them. You can speak for your feelings instead of from them. If you feel sad and hurt, you can pause before responding or go on a walk in nature to gain some insight related to this feeling. You can come back to address the situation later. Rest in the feeling you are having, knowing that feelings, by their very nature, are temporary.

# SECTION 3

## Whole-Person and Healthy Performer

# Chapter 13

# The Six Fundamentals of a Whole-Person and Healthy Performer

No matter who we decide to become and what Choice Identities we nurture, we need to have the healthiest vessel to execute our most challenging goals. When you feel healthy and whole, you can more effectively contribute to whatever team or system you are a part of. You can develop the resiliency and the anti-fragile mind, body, and spirit needed to engage with joy, ease, and composure more readily than when you are not healthy in your mind and body. Negative stresses take a greater toll and are more challenging to bounce back from when you are unhealthy. By effectively managing your energy, you will face life's challenges with clarity, focus, capacity, and capability.

Your team needs your whole self to show up, not a partial version who is unfocused and gives a half-hearted effort because you lack energy due to poor diet, sleep, device management (as in too much social media), or having the skills to manage your emotions. By managing your whole-person energy, you will gain self-mastery and trust in yourself and will be less likely to be thrown off course when things don't go your way. By identifying the necessary tools to manage your physical, emotional, and spiritual energy, you can show up confidently in new, unforeseen, and challenging situations. The six fundamentals of a whole-person and healthy performer will help you recognize what factors may be contributing the most to showing up as the best version of yourself. Most importantly, you will gain an appreciation that being an athlete (or parent, practitioner, administrator or coach) is not the whole of who you are; it's just one of your identities. You have other important roles and identities upon which to rely.

## The Six Fundamentals

Let's look at what could happen if you don't practice the six fundamentals consistently. For example, a father who stays up too late and hence has a grouchy mood and a diminished ability to manage stress at work returns home with an edgy, emotionally unavailable presence. A coach who eats fast food due to convenience and lack of time feels physiologically compromised, then runs a lackluster and disorganized practice where her frustration builds and her temper is short with her athletes, thus eroding trust. A basketball athlete forgets to use breathing techniques to manage his emotions mindfully and then takes his frustrations out on his teammates, lashing out at them when he is upset with himself for missing his last two shots. In a system, these examples of not managing one's energy both hurt the person in their own role and also hurt others who are on the receiving end of the lousy energy management.

Maintaining optimal health in the six fundamentals builds your sense of self-mastery, confidence, and resilience. Physiologically and psychologically, a healthy mind and body can handle more knocks, bumps, and bruises that inevitably occur during practice and competitions. Your mind is responsive to how to solve challenges and bounce back quickly. Volatile emotions, strained and run-down bodies, and fatigued brains and spirits should not be running the show.

In essence, a healthy mind and body make you more resilient. Resilience is the capacity to bounce back. With an unhealthy mind, the struggle to return to a healthier state seems too daunting. In his book *Areté* and his heroic work at (Heroic.us), Brian Johnson talks about three levels of "confidence": fragile, resilient, and anti-fragile.

He uses the metaphor of a box in the mail to explain three levels of confidence. A box labeled "fragile" must be handled with extreme care—just like someone who believes they might break under stress. A "resilient" label suggests the box can take hits and still function, like a person who recovers from hardship. An "anti-fragile" box actually grows stronger the more it's challenged—just as some people become tougher through adversity.

The six fundamentals discussed below will help toughen your vessel while allowing you to recover and bounce forward more powerfully.

Regardless of your role, healthy movement releases built-up tension. A good night's sleep helps us recover physically, cognitively and emotionally. Breathing techniques give us space between stimulus and response so we don't react negatively. Sleep is critical for mood, recovery, learning, memory, movement, decision-making, accuracy, power, and speed. Proper fueling and hydration energize actions and provide health and performance benefits for doing your job and recovering from the cognitive and physical load. Connecting with yourself and others provides meaning, safety, purpose, and a sense of belonging. Communing with nature supports good mental health by helping us connect to the bigger picture and remember what matters. Smelling the grass, hearing birds sing, seeing the scampering of a squirrel, chipmunk, or rabbit, and/or touching the velvety petals of a flower can give us pause to enjoy nature's natural beauty and ease. We remind ourselves that we are of this same natural essence. Whatever happens on a given day can be put into perspective when we connect with nature.

## Proper Breathing

Breathing exercises have existed for thousands of years to promote relaxation, focus, energy, and health. Some religious and spiritual practices, as well as cultural and medical traditions, use breathing exercises to help heal the body, mind, and spirit. Specific breathing practices can foster non-ordinary states of consciousness to facilitate healing and transformation. Life starts and ends with breath. Knowing how to breathe for health and how to breathe for performance are essential for being a whole-person and healthy performer. Because breathing is part of the autonomic nervous system, meaning our bodies do it automatically, we may assume that we don't have to think about it. However, it is important to understand the different types of breathing that can be used to help us in various situations. Dr. Andrew Weil, a renowned integrated whole health physician, recommends breathing as his top foundational health practice.[30]

Before embarking on any breathing exercises, consult your doctor, especially if you have any medical conditions or take any medications that a breathing practice may impact. Additionally, if you are breastfeeding or pregnant, please also consult with your health care professional.

### Nasal breathing

Let's start with the basics of proper breathing. The nose is designed for breathing, and the mouth is designed for eating and communicating. Therefore, breathing should primarily occur in and out of your nose. This does not always happen, however, such as when winded athletes breathe in and out of their mouths. When you can, try to slow down your breathing by inhaling and exhaling from your nose to trigger the release of nitric oxide, thereby enhancing oxygen regulation from red blood cells to tissues. Nitric oxide is a molecule that widens blood vessels and improves oxygen circulation.

An important part of our 24-hour day is breathing correctly during sleep. Those who snore, have sleep apnea, allergies, a deviated septum, or a stuffy nose often unconsciously switch to mouth breathing, resulting in more shallow and less restful sleep. Retraining to nasal breathing throughout the day and finding a way to keep the mouth shut during the night will help you gain better quality sleep, impacting both your performance and health.

## Sleep tape

Some practitioners have recommended using sleep tape to keep the mouth closed during sleep so that nasal breathing becomes the only option. The technique is to place a small strip of athletic, kinesio, or special sleep tape on the mouth to keep it closed during sleep and hence train breathing through the nose continuously during the night. Some people may fear stopping breathing during the night and hence may feel too anxious to try it. Instead, they may focus instead on noticing throughout the day if they're mainly breathing through their nose. Breathing can become more efficient when focused on inhaling and exhaling through the nose, even while exercising. Though it becomes more challenging when doing cardio in zones three or above, retraining your breathing through your nose is still possible. Sleep tape is controversial, so learn what you can about it to see if it's right for you.

## Buteyko breathing method

A method of nasal breathing called the Buteyko breathing method, invented by Russian physician Konstantin Buteyko and popularized by Patrick McKeown, author of *The Oxygen Advantage*, is widely considered to be the most correct method of breathing.[31] This technique increases carbon dioxide levels that trigger oxygen release to your muscles, improving oxygenation levels in your bloodstream. According to research, the average male body has 36 trillion cells and the average female body has 28 trillion, and all of them need oxygen in order to function effectively.[32]

The Buteyko method builds up carbon dioxide in the body, which then drives air hunger or the urge to bring in more oxygen. Oxygenation levels will then increase because carbon dioxide releases oxygen from the bloodstream into the muscles. This method involves very shallow, very slow breathing through your nose. The masters of this method can breathe so slowly and shallowly that their nostril hairs don't move. I find this to be very challenging, but over time you can train yourself to breathe this way, starting with one to five minutes and going up to 10 to 15 minutes. Notice if you breathe through your nose more often throughout the day, with the goal being to do so 100 percent of the time.

An alternate version of this method of oxygenating the body is to practice breath holds called the control pause. While sitting or lying down, breathe normally through your nose for eight to 10 cycles. Then, at the bottom of the exhale, hold your breath in a relaxed manner for as long as you can, aiming to release any tension or resistance throughout the body. The feeling of air hunger will arise, and you will want to breathe. Extend this urge for as long as you can, and when you absolutely can't stand it, let go of the hold and aim to breathe normally and calmly through your nose for a minute. You can do a series of these holds: Completing three to five breath holds over 10 to 15 minutes is an excellent session. Check in on how you feel. You may feel a buzz or a sense of tranquil energy. A healthy breath hold is 45–60 seconds, but you may need to build up to this over time. Free divers are known for being able to hold their breath for over three or four minutes after a great deal of training. Additional benefits of this breathing include reducing stress and anxiety and improving conditions such as sleep apnea and asthma. However, you should consult your doctor regarding any contraindications.

## Alternate nostril breathing

Other forms of nasal breathing include the yogic practice of alternate nostril breathing. This method involves alternating between breathing in one nostril, closing that nostril off with your finger or thumb, and exhaling out the opposite nostril. Then, switch sides by breathing back into the nostril that you just exhaled out of, closing it off, and exhaling out of the nostril with which you started. Continuing this way for five to 20 minutes results in a more balanced-feeling brain and a sense of clarity and calm.

You can also practice by focusing on breathing in and out of the left nostril (known as Ida Nadi breathing in Sanskrit). Close your right nostril with your finger. Focus on left-nostril breathing to stimulate more creativity and intuition by activating the brain's right hemisphere. You can also practice breathing in and out of the right nostril (called Pingala Nadi breathing) to activate the left hemisphere which is associated with stimulating a more rational, logical, and structured approach.

All three methods are exercises that are part of the practice of pranayama, a Sanskrit word meaning "control of" or "to direct life force." Honoring ancient history and wisdom using breathing methods directs our life force and is an important practice for a whole person and a healthy performer.

## Sleeping

The number one game changer in performance and health is the quality, duration and consistency of sleep. All physical and mental health markers trace back to sleep, as many essential mechanisms and processes occur during this process. Unfortunately, with the advent of artificial light, 24-hour entertainment on various devices, and FOMO, human sleep across the planet and in every generation has suffered widely.

Aim to keep a consistent sleep-wake cycle such that you are awake and asleep within 15–30 minutes of your typical times of putting your head on the pillow and waking up, even on weekends. The magic sleep hours to keep your circadian rhythms consistent are from 10 p.m. to 4 a.m. If you are going to take a nap, doing so before 3 p.m. and keeping the duration less than 60 minutes will help build your sleep drive. Having seven to nine hours of sleep per night works for most people, adding one to two hours if you are training intensely at an elite level (either by taking a nap or extending your nighttime sleep period). Sleep is not just about quantity, as the quality and consistency of sleep also matters in improving your health and performance.

Maintain nighttime routines to help your body and mind prepare for rest. Make sure your room is cold, dark, and quiet. You can also practice the three-two-one method, for timing your activities: Three hours before bed, stop eating food; two hours before bed, stop doing work; and one hour before bed, stop interacting with devices. Work with the natural light-dark cycles of the day to balance your circadian rhythm, being sure to get 10–15 minutes of natural light exposure from the outside as soon as possible upon waking.

## Mood

Sleep matters so much because it influences our mood, muscle repair, movement, and memory. We have all met or been irritable grouches when we did not get enough sleep. Chronic sleep deprivation and insomnia are associated with low mood that can impact emotional regulation, decision-making, and productivity, and are also associated with mental health disorders such as anxiety, depression, bipolar disorder, and ADHD. This association can be bi-directional, such that mental health disorders affect one's quality of sleep and lack of sleep affects the symptoms of mental health disorders. Getting good sleep also improves academic and athletic performance and the health of relationships.

## Muscle repair

Performance recovery and the role of sleep in helping with muscle repair is an important consideration. Running around with no rest and stating, "I'll sleep when I'm dead" should not be viewed as a badge of honor. Rest and recovery, with sleep as the focus, holds evidence as being the primary driver of muscle repair and growth that occurs after training. During sleep, HGH (human growth hormone) is released, which is involved in protein synthesis and the repair and development of new muscle tissue. Moreover, glycogen storages are replenished during sleep so muscles recover and will have the necessary energy stores for next-day performances. Other hormones are re-balanced and inflammation is reduced during sleep, further contributing to recovery.

## Movement

Having good sleep quality over consecutive days results in better movement. Movement includes speed, accuracy, and decision-making, using information processing to calculate what and how much speed, distance, effort, and precision is needed to apply a skill, move, or play. So with proper sleep, you have more power, speed, and accuracy of decisions, both physically and cognitively. High-level cognition processes are enhanced, and reaction times become faster.

## Memory

Memories are consolidated during sleep. What is learned during the day at practice, work, school, home, or with friends is consolidated at night during sleep. All our work, effort, and experiences, whether intended or unintended, would be for naught with poor sleep quality, but getting adequate sleep can improve memory recall and retention by up to 40 percent.

# Fueling and Hydrating

My perspective on fueling and hydrating is to keep it simple and whole, focusing on unprocessed nutrition sources as much as possible. The advent of the internet, social media, and influencers has made the field of nutrition confusing and contradictory. Every body is different and experiences different demands, stresses, and inner workings, so there's no one-size-fits-all approach to nutrition or diet.

You may have particular allergies, sensitivities, likes, and dislikes. Work within those parameters while recognizing that not liking vegetables or fruits may be because you have not trained your taste buds. Working with a licensed and experienced dietitian can help ensure that your body receives the nutrients it needs for optimum functioning and health. I recommend finding a certified holistic nutritionist or registered dietitian who can do functional testing. But regardless of your individual needs, real food as opposed to processed food is better for everyone. You will perform and feel better when you consume nature's food and drink.

If you're a younger athlete or adult, you may be able to get away with a non-nutritious diet in the short run but playing the long game of what's best for your body, mind, and emotions will ultimately serve you better. What you do now impacts you 5, 10, and 20 years from now. Thinking long-term may be challenging, but it is helpful to remain mindful of the long-term impacts of your short-term decisions without obsessing about them.

## Seven practices for fueling and hydrating

While everyone is different, these basic guidelines of what to consume daily, how to eat, and what to avoid are a good place to start. Let the magic of the number seven lead the way:

- seven to nine cups of organic veggies and fruits
  - reach for nature's bright foods that reflect the rich colors of the rainbow versus white foods
  - berries, greens, and yams are rich in color and antioxidants, which help reduce inflammation

- aim for half a plate full of colorful produce at breakfast, lunch, and dinner
- seven healthy fats
  - choose olive oil, coconut oil, tallow, organic butter, avocado, oily fish, whole nuts and seeds, and dark chocolate
  - avoid inflammatory oils like vegetable, soy, canola, and corn
- seven responsible proteins
  - select meats from animals raised on regenerative, climate-friendly organic farms
  - grass-fed only beef, free-range foraging birds, eggs, wild-caught fish (not farm raised), organic rice and beans, lentils, nut butters, and dairy as tolerated (such as Greek yogurt and cottage cheese)
  - other sources of protein can include eggs, tofu, and sustainably harvested wild seafood.
  - Vegan or vegetarian eaters can consult with a professional for their best recommendations
- seven grams or less of added sugar (ideally zero grams)
  - the more you eliminate sugar, the less you crave it
  - pause for seven minutes to give yourself time to choose an alternative to eating foods with processed sugar
  - add fat and/or protein when eating something with added sugar to reduce the sugar spike
  - eliminate sugary drinks
  - sweeteners like stevia, honey, maple syrup, and coconut sugar are healthier alternatives
- seven processed or packaged foods to minimize or eliminate
  - chips, candy, cookies, crackers, cereals, donuts, processed meats with nitrate additives (such as cold cuts, bacon, and sausages)
  - read labels if the food comes in a package; there should be seven or fewer ingredients that you can easily pronounce

- drink 70 ounces or more of spring water with natural minerals
  - drink slowly and steadily throughout the day
  - two large gulps are approximately four ounces, so four large gulps per hour for nine hours will get you to 70 ounces
  - your weight in pounds divided in half is the number of ounces of water you need for health maintenance (e.g. a 150-pound person needs 75 ounces of water)
- take 7 minutes x 3 or more to eat (e.g. 21 minutes)
  - take your time; chew your food and slow down while eating, enjoying and experiencing the texture, complexity of tastes, temperature, aroma, visual appeal, context, ambiance, occasion, sounds, consistency, and emotions
  - chew thoroughly before swallowing; rest your fork down for seven seconds between bites

### Seven rules for fueling and hydrating

Continuing with the magic of number seven, use these seven simple rules when it comes to fueling and hydrating effectively.

1. Eat most of your food from trees, plants, bushes, and the Earth. Nature has a phenomenal way of balancing nutritional needs with humans' needs for optimal mind, body, and emotional functioning. What you ingest affects the entire functioning of your body. Sugary, heavily processed, machine-made foods impact your mood, thinking, attention, digestion, energy, and sleep. Every cell in your body matters and is helped or hurt by what you consume.

2. Read food labels. Due to the time-saving convenience of grocery stores, most people no longer grow their own food. It is important to read labels to discern whether what is in the packaged food is what you want to put in your body. All cells in your body will

eventually be impacted by what you serve them. If you cannot pronounce or understand what is in the packaging, returning the item to the shelf may be best. Look for packaged foods with ingredients that you know and understand. If the item has added sugar, it should be in its more natural form, such as honey, coconut, or pure cane sugar. Eat sweets with healthier fats, fiber, and protein to blunt blood sugar spikes.

3. Consider the environmental impacts of your choices. If you eat an animal, you eat what the animal eats. The more natural, gentle, and aligned the practices of raising the animals, the better those foods will be for your body and for the animal.

4. Combine different foods, such as eating fibrous foods with protein and fats. Your body will naturally digest foods to glean the nutrition it needs. Foods harmonize to make nutrition exponentially more valuable. For example: Eating fibrous, carbohydrate-rich foods like sweet potatoes along with butter or healthy fats, asparagus, greens, and protein, such as chicken, fish, or red meat, provides a power punch of rich antioxidants and nutrients that both heal and energize the body while keeping glucose spikes at a low and steady release.

5. Spice it up: Use herbs and spices as your natural flavorings to keep your food interesting and appealing. Don't be afraid to play with testing combinations of different spices. The compounding effects of spices and herbs, adding nutrients, antioxidants, flavor, and fun, make the effort to learn about them worthwhile.

6. Go nuts! Raw and sprouted nuts, seeds, beans, and legumes offer healthy fats, protein, and fiber for sustained energy. You can add nuts and seeds to salads or enjoy them as a snack. Beans and rice make a whole protein, so animal and seafood sources do not have to be your sole protein sources.

7.  Stay hydrated with water, electrolytes, and minerals. Among the trillions of cells in our bodies, the most abundant molecule is water (constituting 70 percent of our body)! Water, made up of hydrogen and oxygen, is the most essential molecule required for life on Earth. Humans cannot survive on water alone, however; electrolytes and minerals, such as sodium, potassium, calcium, magnesium, and phosphate, are essential to cell function (see Appendix B for recommended products to stay hydrated).

## Moving

Movement seems to be an obvious factor when discussing fundamental health and performance behaviors in athletes and other performers. Many might argue that it is the number one behavior of athletes since all sports require movement, and it's the area to which most athletes, coaches, and practitioners turn first to make performance gains. "*Citius, Altius, Fortius*" is the Olympic motto that means "Faster, Higher, Stronger," which are verbs that are commonly related to movement.

Moving, for any human, is not just about athletic movement. If the concept of movement was a shape, it would be a large circle in which the smaller circles of training, conditioning, practicing, skill development, and competing are all encompassed. Humans are designed to move. Movement includes activities of daily living such as getting up and down from sitting and lying to walking, reaching, balancing, stretching, standing, and taking the stairs. Movement is required to escape danger, stay safe and alive, and keep the body, mind, and spirit healthy, active, and alert. The opposite of movement is stagnation, languishing, and sedentariness.

Countless books have been written on the importance of exercise, how to train more efficiently and effectively, and how to gain strength, power, speed, agility, balance, flexibility, endurance, and mobility. These are all competencies that any athlete needs to maintain top form and technique and to make accurate decisions under the speed and pressure of competition. What has received less attention for athletes, however, is that movement also affects clarity of mind, mood management, the health of your cells outside of competition and training, and the health of your DNA. Movement trumps one or two hours of training if you are sedentary for the remaining 12–14 hours of the day because movement helps your overall health functioning while training is for helping you execute your sports skills. Of course, movement and all of the healthy performer fundamentals are not just for athletes but also for coaches, parents, and TAT members. The healthier each part of the system is, the healthier the whole system becomes.

Walking in nature, also called forest bathing, is scientifically supported to improve mood, boost your immune system, reduce stress, and offer other health benefits.[33] The practice of forest bathing, popularized by Dr. Qing Li, is more than just walking in the woods.[34] It's a practice that mindfully engages all five senses. Forest bathing includes at least three of the healthy performer fundamentals: deliberate breathing, moving, and communing with nature. You could add another fundamental if you brought nourishing food and hydration products. If you bring a friend or loved one or reflect on a relationship, you can also include socioemotional connecting. If you add a 20-minute nap on a picnic blanket in the forest, you can check off addressing all six fundamentals!

## Connecting

Emotions and feelings are complex and highly personal and are often temporary. We often cannot control which feelings may arise in us, but we can choose how to respond mindfully and learn to control how we react. Learning how to manage emotions mindfully is a skill of socioemotional connecting, and understanding your own emotions will help you more mindfully connect with others.

Humans are social creatures; we are meant to be a part of communities, families, and friend groups as members of various social units. We rely on each other for food, shelter, and support. Currently, however, more people across generations are socially isolated, lonely, and living alone than ever before. According to the US census in 2020, more than 27 percent of the population lives in a single-person household, compared with 7.7 percent in 1940.[35] The physical and mental health risks of loneliness and social isolation can be alarming. Loneliness is the subjective and usually unwanted feeling of separateness, whereas social isolation is an objective physical separation from others. Socioemotional connecting is an act of self-preservation, and preservation of the "other" and the "group." It is the thread that joins a group in a common bond. People who actively engage in meaningful conversations and productive activities with others tend to have a greater sense of purpose, better health, better moods, increased cognitive functioning, and overall higher well-being. Aspects of healthy relating and authentic connection to oneself and others include: socioemotional connecting, positive relationships, internally connecting to and naming emotions, doing body scans, responding with beneficial intentions, slowing down, putting phones away during interactions, and eating meals together with ease and joy.

Sports teams and athletic environments can be primary ways to socialize, connect, and meet the emotional-support needs of belonging and feeling part of something bigger than yourself. Moreover, working together, collaborating, challenging, and helping each other grow in pursuit of bigger goals helps develop your confidence as a contributing team member. Utilizing and offering your unique strengths, gifts, and talents to help and connect with others increases self-esteem, self-acceptance, and self-worth.

## Communing with Nature

A way to return to your natural self, your Human-First identity, is to return to the spiritual home of nature from whence you came. Being immersed in nature often generates a sense of awe and gratitude for the beauty we see and the connection we feel in belonging to and being accepted as part of something bigger than ourselves. Being in nature can help us focus less on our self-interested thoughts because nature is inclusive of many things.

Our perspective expands when we tap into nature's spaciousness and tune into quiet and stillness. Our minds experience more clarity when we can be present in nature without all the clamor of modern life. There is evidence that reconnecting with nature, even seeing pictures and videos of natural scenes, reduces stress, helps with physical and mental recovery, and triggers positive emotions and a sense of belonging.[36] Being in nature also provides significant health benefits via physical movement, cleaner air, and more reverence and awe, leading to greater longevity.

I know people who prefer the hustle and bustle of city life, feeling stimulated by the speed of activity, noise, excitement, number of people, conveniences, and choices that a city offers. They may find nature to be boring, unsettling, or unsafe. However, some research studies showed that people who lived close to green spaces experienced reduced symptoms of ADHD and reported greater social acceptance and connection, more civility, less violence, and a greater sense of protection of their neighbors and community members than those who did not live near green spaces.[37] [38]

Ultimately, all the six fundamentals of a whole-person and healthy performer help reduce or prevent the likelihood of physical, mental, or emotional injuries and accelerate the recovery process from such injuries. All six fundamentals complement each other and are intended to help you own yourself as a whole, already naturally perfect being and a healthy performer.

These six fundamentals are the keys to improving mental and physical health and performance. They can be paired and combined. When the whole PACT system is optimized in the six fundamentals, everyone wins.

# SECTION 4
## The Confident Performer

# Chapter 14

# The Skills of Confidence and Focus

Mental skills are not evident most of the time, making them hard to mimic, but they are needed just as much as physical skills. The core four mental skills (plus one) are: Deliberate breathing, self-talk plus body language, goal or intention setting, and mental rehearsal. The plus one skill is gratitude and reflection so that learning can take place. The more a person uses the skills together, the more synchronous and exponential their power and impact can become. What's exciting about the Core Four mental skills (plus one) is that each skill is immediately usable anytime, anywhere, under any circumstance, and by anyone. Moreover, others may or may not know whether you are using them. You may witness a swimmer deliver a big exhale using deliberate breathing to relieve tension before stepping onto the diving blocks. On the tennis court, you might see a player look at her strings and mouth some words to herself. On the field, you might see a soccer player roll his shoulders back and look up to trigger his confidence after setting up the ball for a direct kick.

If mental skills, like physical skills, were even more apparent and we could witness the great athletes using them, mental skills utilization would go viral. It may be more apparent when athletes don't utilize mental skills in certain pressure moments. For example, an observer might notice fear on the face of an inexperienced baseball player stepping up to bat, who might be holding tension in their shoulders, clenching their jaw, furrowing their eyebrows, or looking like they are almost holding their breath. A high school basketball player's embarrassment may be evident in his body language, such as slumped shoulders, head-shaking, and jogging slowly back to defense while looking down at the ground after his three-pointer falls short of the basket.

The Core Four (plus one) mental skills are for everyone in the Winning System. Parents can benefit from listening to their self-talk to determine whether it is helping or hindering them when their athlete-child is late and can't find their cleats. A coach can use deliberate breathing to help gain clarity before giving a half-time talk to get her players' heads back in the game against a weaker opponent when the score is down. A coach might pause to consider whether yelling at the players is most beneficial to turn the game around or if it would be better to relieve their stress with some lightness before reminding them of who they are and what kind of team they are. An athlete might use mental rehearsal in the locker room before the match to review his mental highlight reel and remind himself that he is prepared, can play the game well, and that today is just another day to give his best effort. Even a member of the TAT might use breathing and self-talk techniques to handle a formidable injury and calm an athlete writhing in pain. An athletic trainer preparing her lacrosse athletes for practice in a busy training room might use deliberate breathing and self-talk to stay focused and respond appropriately to the athletes who have the highest needs or correct athletes who are being disruptive.

## Deliberate Breathing

The first mental skill I teach any performer is deliberate breathing, also known as breathing for performance. I covered breathing methods that focused more on health in the six fundamentals of a whole-person and healthy performer. These deliberate breathing skills are specifically to bring focus and clarity before and during performance. Breathing for performance is the most straightforward, accessible, and trainable skill that anyone can learn quickly and experience immediate benefits from. It still surprises me when I hear from a range of adults from young to older that they have never heard of using the breath to help manage emotions in the moment, such as pausing to take a deep breath. Breathing is the first thing that is checked for when assessing signs of life. The breath (prana) is the life force, without which there is no life. To gain control of your physiology, start with your breath.

Athletes train their breathing to put them into a flow state to perform optimally during practice, training, and competition. Parents and coaches use breathing to calm themselves so they can reassure their child or athlete and respond with loving kindness while holding them to high standards. Depression, self-loathing, and a focus on mistakes live in the past, whereas anxiety and worry live in the future, so neither exists in the present moment. Deliberately focusing on your breath takes you immediately to the present moment, where typically we are able to recognize that we are actually OK and can feel a little bit better.

Although we breathe automatically without thinking, deliberate breathing is a skill, as you need to pay attention to your breath to center or quiet the mind. A breathing-for-performance practice lends itself to "being present for what is, without judgment, in an open-hearted way," as said by Jack Kornfield, a world-renowned Buddhist psychologist.[39] Similar to a mindfulness practice, breathing helps us get to a more mindful state of being in the present without attachment or judgment. Deliberate breathing takes training and consistent practice so that you can remember to focus on your breath when you need it most.

There is an intended purpose for each breathing technique, and each may have a different impact. You may like some techniques more than others, but I suggest giving each method at least five minutes of focus over four to six separate sessions to determine its effects on you. As with any skill, it takes a great deal of practice under various conditions before the technique becomes reliably available in your toolbox.

You may not like a particular technique at all, but this is a wonderful opportunity to go deeper to see if you can determine why you are experiencing such resistance to it. For me, the Buteyko method is the hardest. I fight it and find myself craving a deep, long inhale, even when I intend to practice with patience and persistence. Whichever technique bothers or challenges you the most may be just the one to work on mastering over time. As you train yourself to do hard things while you breathe through them, your anti-fragile confidence will increase and your capacity and stability under pressure will solidify.

The other experience most people have when first learning to focus on their breath is that the mind wanders like a puppy in obedience training. The experienced dog trainer gently guides the puppy back to the obedience skill they are working on, and after repeated efforts, rewards, and corrections, the puppy learns to stay still for more extended periods of time. An inexperienced trainer who does not understand how to help the puppy learn would over-correct and punish them, making training a miserable and unrewarding experience for both puppy and human! So, let's not do that to ourselves. When you are learning a new skill over time, use patience and persistence to gently bring yourself back to the task at hand. Work in short bursts and take mental breaks mixed with playtime, just as you would with a puppy in training.

If I were to teach only one performance and health technique, I would teach proper breathing and types of breathing methods for different purposes. Here, I will share with you the primary techniques I teach to athletes. If you find these techniques interesting, I invite you to explore this fascinating field further.

The book *Breath: The New Science of a Lost Art* by James Nestor is a fascinating resource on the power of breathing.[40] Nestor's work with Patrick McKeown has made breathing into a mainstream topic, along with discussing the scientific rationale for and benefits of knowing how to breathe more efficiently and retraining poor breathing patterns. McKeown's and Nestor's work, along with that of others such as Anders Olsson, Belisa Vranrich, Richard Brown and Patricia Gerberg, Al Lee, and Don Campbell, have all contributed to the literature, science, and body of work on how breathing can help anyone improve their performance and health.[41] [42] [43] [44] Free divers and big wave surfers exemplify athletes who extensively train their lungs through breath-hold training. Be sure to work with an experienced practitioner for your safety and well-being.

## The 4-7-8 and 4-7-1 methods

Pre-performance breathing methods include Dr. Andrew Weil's popularized method, the 4-7-8 breathing, which the Cleveland Clinic and other medical organizations have touted. Its numbers are nothing more than the counts, or seconds, used to guide how long you inhale, hold your breath, and exhale. In the 4-7-8 method, you inhale for four seconds, hold for seven seconds, and exhale for 8 seconds. For some, this is very challenging as the buildup of carbon dioxide during the hold and the exhalation triggers the urge to breathe.

The 4-7-1 technique is simply a variation of the 4-7-8, except in this method, you will inhale for four seconds, exhale for seven seconds, and hold at the bottom of the exhale for one second. The extended exhalation triggers the rest and digestion of the parasympathetic nervous system to calm anxious feelings and focus the mind on counting the length of the inhales and exhales. The mind may want to toggle rapidly to other thoughts, but the practice is to maintain your focus only on the counts and the breathing cycles.

You may need to adjust the lengths of your inhales and exhales as you build carbon dioxide tolerance and expand your capacity to lengthen and strengthen your breath cycles. These two methods are excellent ways to start rhythmically counting your inhale and exhale lengths while simultaneously counting the rounds of breath. Start with 10 rounds, with one round consisting of a full inhale, exhale, and a hold. If you get distracted, gently start again at round one until you reach 10 rounds without your mind wandering off like the puppy in training. Once you have reached 10 rounds, build your capacity by five rounds until you reach 30 rounds without your mind wandering or losing count. You may find that you notice more easily throughout the day whenever you are breathing shallowly, are distracted, or unconsciously holding your breath. Without anyone knowing, you can practice your simple, intentional breathing to bring yourself back to the present moment and refocus your intention. This is a fantastic and simple tool you can use anywhere, anytime, on your own, throughout your self-mastery adventure, and if you have given it the practice and attention it deserves, you may find it handy to go to your breath at the most critical and challenging times you face.

### Box breathing (4-4-4-4 Technique)

Box breathing is a wonderful focusing technique where each part of the breath equates to the four equal sides of a box. Some athletes like to imagine a box to keep their focus, visualizing each side of the box as they inhale for four counts, hold their breath for four counts, exhale for four counts, and hold at the bottom for four counts. Continue this way for at least five rounds and notice whether you notice any changes in your mood, sense of focus, ease in your body, and/or peace of mind.

I first learned about box breathing when I was preparing to work with the Green Berets of the 7th Special Forces Group at Eglin Air Force Base in the panhandle area of Florida. I have found that male athletes, clients, and soldiers seem to be more attracted to box breathing than females.

### The Wim Hof method

Wim Hof, the eccentric and fascinating Dutchman known as "The Iceman," popularized his breathing method by achieving incredible human feats and setting world records. He is known for setting a world record of immersing himself in ice to his neck for 2 hours and 11 minutes and using his breathing technique to maintain his core body temperature. Two feats of his that I found most impressive were reaching 22,000 feet on Mount Everest in shorts and shoes, and running a marathon in the Namib Desert in Southern Africa for five hours and 45 minutes without drinking a drop of water amidst air temperatures of 104°F. These are not feats that I recommend for others to attempt or beat, but it is impressive that he was capable of these achievements using his methods of cold exposure, breathing techniques, and changing his mindset using meditation.

The Wim Hof breathing method consists of vigorous and rapid inhales with easy, natural exhales before vigorously inhaling again. For each set, he performs 20 to 30 rounds (inhaling and exhaling constitutes one round) before holding his breath at the bottom of his 20th or 30th exhale for as long as he can while completely relaxing and letting go of any tension or anticipation. Wim Hof recommends that you lie down during this exercise in case of light-headedness or dizziness. Doing three sets of 30 vigorous inhales paired with easy natural exhales and extended breath holds after each set is a great session.[45] His methods are not without controversy, however, so approaching this method with caution is recommended.

The steps for using this method are as follows:

- Inhale vigorously through the nose or mouth, taking in as much oxygen as possible. Then, let go of the breath through the mouth or nose without pushing the air out. Repeat 20–30 times.
- At the bottom of the 20th or 30th exhale, hold your breath in a very relaxed manner, and extend your breath hold for as long as possible. You might experience the mammalian reflex, which drives oxygen further into the muscles, as a jerky sensation where the urge to breathe is at its highest. You do not need to take yourself this far. Do this only under supervision and with a trained and experienced practitioner.
- Repeat this sequence three times.

When I teach the Wim Hof method to athletes, I ask them whether they think they could do more push-ups while breathing or holding their breath. Almost 100 percent of the time, the number of push-ups they think they can do while holding their breath is fewer than the number they think they can do while breathing. I then take these athletes through the above Wim Hof method techniques. After the third round of breathing, when they start the breath hold, I have them flip over immediately and pump out as many good-quality push-ups as they can while holding their breath. They individually stop the activity when they urgently need to breathe and can no longer hold their breath even if their teammates are still going.

The vast majority of the time, the athletes pump out more push-ups while holding their breath than the number they'd said they could do while breathing, sometimes doing two to five times more push-ups than they thought they could do while holding their breath! This experience is quite a revelation for most athletes about appreciating the power of breathing exercises and oxygenating the body. The breath holds help oxygenate their muscles, providing them with more energy and focus.

Tummo breathing, similar to the Wim Hof method, also helps to heat the body and control core temperature. It is a great method to use before stepping into a cold shower or ice bath. Focus on your breathing while in the cold water but for safety reasons, do not do the breath holds. I recommend also exploring other breathing techniques to help focus your mind and oxygenate your body prior to performance, such as Kapalabhati breathing, Lion's breath, the physiological sigh, and humming breath.

## Internal and External Dialogue

Who do you talk to and hear from most? A parent? Coworker? A sibling? Your friends? Regardless of your answer, you're actually the person you talk to the most throughout your day. A recent study by Dr. Jordan Poppenk and Julie Tseng out of Queen's University in Canada estimates that our thoughts change about 6,200 times per day, averaging 6.5 thought changes per minute.[46] These brain worms are the threads of your self-talk, the patterns of your thoughts. Most of these daily thoughts occur with no other person in your life except yourself!

Are your thoughts and internal dialogue helping or hindering you? If you ask most people in the United States and even globally whether they are experiencing more stress now than say 10 or more years ago, they will probably agree that they are experiencing more stress today due to global, economic, climate, and social uncertainty. Without conscious intervention, we will keep thinking the same things and telling ourselves the same stories, which are often unkind and unhelpful. Fortunately, we can take action to change these detrimental patterns.

*Self-Talk*

What would happen if you admitted to yourself that you're having the same thoughts day after day, and that may be undermining your state of mind and body? Reflect on these four scenarios of what you might be saying to yourself or to others the great majority of the time, and ask, Does this dialogue tend to be helpful or hindering; critical or encouraging?

- What do you say internally about yourself? How often are your internal thoughts kind and supportive of yourself?
- What do you say to yourself about other people or about circumstances and events? Do they tend to be more often kind and supportive or negative and critical?
- What do you say out loud to others about yourself? Are the words you say out loud about yourself to others something you told yourself before you said it out loud to others?
- What do you say out loud to others about other people? Are the words something you told yourself before you said it out loud to others?

Do you tend to build yourself or others up? Do you look for the good in people, or do you tend to tear down, criticize, or put down situations, people, and events? In these conversations with yourself or others, do you feel better and more energized by these internal and external conversations? Regardless of whether the situations are true or not, are the conversations helpful to or hindering progress? How do you feel afterward? If your conversations tend to be more negative, it may seem like you feel better in the moment after venting your feelings by putting someone else down behind their back, but have you noticed how your inner self feels later? Do you feel superior or just irritated about other people? Could your complaints about others be reflective of how you feel about yourself?

How do you feel after you have built yourself up or talked positively about someone you admire? Sincerely and authentically finding the good in yourself and others tends to result in positive feelings, induces a more relaxed state, and encourages hope for better things to come. When working with the director of UPenn's Center for Positive Psychology, Dr. Karen Reivich, I have heard her say to audiences of coaches and athletes, "Hunt the good stuff." When we do so, our feelings of hope, optimism, and health increase while our feelings of anxiety, depression, isolation, and loneliness decrease. This practice is not just a suggestion, it's a beacon of hope for a brighter mental landscape.

The nature of thoughts is spontaneous, ceaseless, and unpredictable. You might say, "That was random; where did that thought come from?" And then wonder, "If I thought it, then it must be true," or "I should act on it." We can quiet our minds, re-direct our thoughts, and stay open and curious about what arises in our minds, but we never fully stop thinking while we are alive. Our brains are constantly processing information, and when we accept that the very nature of thoughts is that they are spontaneous, ceaseless, and unpredictable, then we don't have to overthink them. Hence, we should try to pause before responding or speaking and ask if what we are about to say to ourselves or others will help or hinder health and performance. Try to hunt for the good and change your thoughts to more beneficial ones or rest with them with nothing needing to be done. When your thoughts are helpful, celebrate and acknowledge the good stuff!

More often than I cared to experience, my leadership coach in Evergreen, Colorado, Jim Anderson, held up the mirror of truth to me, and I rarely liked what I saw. My thoughts about myself and others were getting in the way of seeing clearly and accepting reality as it is. What I most often complained about was something I did to myself or to others consistently. The mirror taught me to look inward first. He would erupt into boisterous laughter when the lightbulb went off in my head, and soon I learned to laugh with him.

## Affirmations

Affirmations, which are repeated statements that can help shift your perspective on reality and create new beliefs, are your tools of empowerment. Beliefs are just the thoughts we keep thinking. We repeat our thoughts about how we think the world works, what other people are like, what we think of ourselves, and what's possible or not possible. We often accept thoughts and beliefs as they are without testing their truth, but by using affirmations, you can take control and shape your beliefs.

Affirmations are thoughts or statements we design. When repeated with authentic emotion, affirmations have the power to shift deep-seated beliefs, which then impact your feelings and views, influencing your actions or lack of action. However, the fastest way to change your beliefs is to change your actions, which can immediately change your mind. Waiting for your beliefs to change can take a long time, whereas taking action strikes beliefs right at their core. For example, if you are scared to jump off the 10M platform into a pool, your mind may tell you that you can't do it, that you are scared. The more you wait, delay, and anticipate the jump, the more scared you get. Instead, if you have witnessed other people jump off without delay, you too can decide to just jump off without delay. Then doing the action itself changes your mind about whether you can do it or not.

The science behind self-talk and affirmations lies in neuroplasticity, which means that your brain is flexible and adaptable. New neuronal pathways are paved when you repeatedly start talking to yourself differently than you have done previously. Think of your self-talk as a type of habit or like a physical skill. Your habits become ingrained from repeating the behavior, like brushing your teeth before bed. Just as your physical skills improve when you practice them with consistency and intent, so can your self-talk and therefore your beliefs, such that your new helpful habits eventually become more automatic. These skills also apply to people with whom you may be in conflict. Consider what you are saying to yourself or others about them, and whether the self-talk is enhancing or hindering your relationship. Let go of whether something is true or not true and focus on whether what you are telling yourself is helping or hindering.

What if someone else talked to you the way you speak to yourself? Would you feel encouraged or discouraged? Would you ever talk to your friend in the same way you talk to yourself? Most people would not want someone else to speak to them the way they talk to themselves! Strengthening your neuropathways by weakening the connections of negative self-talk helps you perform more easily. You focus instead on what is helping, not hindering. Like turning up the volume of the TV in one room while turning down the volume of the radio playing in the adjacent room, by using affirmations and power words, you can bolster your confidence.

Complete the sentences below to get started on creating your affirmations.

- I'm the kind of person who _____.
- My future Self needs me to _____.
- My team gets the best from me when I _____.
- My bright future holds the possibility of _____.
- My daily tactics to ensure a growth mindset include_____.

## Power words

Power words are single words or short phrases to use while performing to train your mind to help you, not hinder you. For example, if you are lifting weights, you might repeat, "Strong," "I got this," "Explode," or "Powerful." In contrast, if you are telling yourself how hard it is, that you are not sure you can do it, or that you are too tired, your mind shuts down your body even when there is more in your tank. An untrained mind quits before the body does.

Have you ever been in a situation when you physically stopped early because your mind said you could not do any more, and then realized, you probably could have done more? Certainly, your muscles and other bodily functions were sending signals of fatigue, and for self-preservation and safety to prevent catastrophic injury, your brain sent signals back to your body to "shut it down." The complex mechanisms have not been completely studied and mapped out. Rest assured, you likely have a bit more in the tank than you may be giving yourself credit for, and self-talk can help convince your brain to not shut down the body … yet.

Self-talk can help you be more powerful, endure for longer, and get more reps or lift heavier weights. If while sprinting you tell yourself to keep the lead or close the gap, you can push your body to maintain or increase speed. While training on the US field hockey team, I developed a stack of index cards with power words written on each card, such as, "lightning quick," "confident," "clear, concise communication," "powerful," "strong," "skillful," "explosive," and "save!" As a mental warm-up before every practice and match, I would review each index card, close my eyes, and envision myself playing like the card described. I used power words as cues or triggers to generate an image in my mind's eye. This consistent, pre-practice routine and mental warm-up made the difference between me finally making the World Cup, Pan American Games, and Olympic teams, instead of being sidelined yet again.

Powerful words can also help you refocus your mind more quickly after a mistake by redirecting the brain to a simple task so your body can be ready for the more complicated actions of the next play or action. When the mind gets too busy, the body can get confused about what the mind actually wants, which is a common mental complaint from athletes called "overthinking." For example, golfers can have too many swing thoughts, which affects their timing, power, and accuracy. Basketball players can have too many shooting thoughts, which interferes with the relaxation needed to flow and make the shot. As you become more masterful and efficient with your physical skills, your self-talk, power words, and phrases may become more simple and specific. Simple thoughts help you maintain your focus on the right things so your body can do complex actions.

## Short moments

The Short Moments Team offers a new way of using the mind. Three of the most common reactions involving people, circumstances, events, or sensations that may arise in one's life are indulging, avoiding, or attempting to replace an experience. Whether positive, negative, or neutral, without knowing an alternative, the conventional reaction is an attempt to neutralize mental, emotional, or physical pain.

Here are a few examples of the three conventional reactions to triggering or uncomfortable experiences:

- **indulge:** exaggerate, dramatize, make bigger, overthink, and ruminate about "how bad or good" the experience, person (s), or events are.
- **avoid:** pretend it's not a problem, dismiss, reject, evade, or not acknowledge "the unpleasantness" or compliment it.
- **correct:** apply overly positive antidotes or attempt to frantically alter and reorganize the person, situation or event so they are more tolerable.

But a new way of using the mind as a solution for relating with any type of experience, person or event is to simply:

- **rest** with relaxed openness. As situations, people, and events arise, the most easeful and simple response is to rely on complete openness. Any type of improvement from this vantage point comes from the clarity of openness. A coach might relax and consider what might be most beneficial without having to fix an athlete. A parent might address a coach with complete ease and curiosity. An athlete might relax and consider their own areas of improvement without judgment, instead of indulging with thoughts about how the coach doesn't know anything. Sit with and face reality, instead of arguing against it. Allow everything to be as it is to recognize ease and spontaneous benefit as the actual nature of all experiences, moment by moment.

The optimal way to rest is to allow "people, circumstances, events, and sensations" to be as they are without needing to replace, avoid, or indulge. Rest does not necessarily mean sitting on the couch and doing nothing, but instead going about one's day, emphasizing relaxed openness. Rather than investing in unnecessary tension, reactions, flamboyance, irritations, frustrations, resistance, or arguments. It is beneficial for your well-being and that of everyone to rest with, be at ease with, and respond to situations in a solution-oriented manner with the natural stability of wisdom, compassion, and openness.[47]

The simple practice to "rest for short moments repeatedly until they become continuous" can be practiced by anyone at any time.[48] Rest is the ultimate form of composure under pressure or stress. Relaxed openness taps into the basic nature of the mind by connecting with naturally powerful and beneficial intelligence, which is the essence of your identity; your ever-present natural intelligence. The sense of relief you feel immediately, and as practice on which to rely, is nothing short of profound.

## Body Language and Power Poses

Have you ever observed someone's body language? It speaks volumes about who they are and how others see them. For example, a person who strides forward with confidence holding their shoulders back and chest up, not their nose up, exudes an air of ease and relaxation, is perceived as more attractive, intelligent, and possessing leadership qualities. This underscores the significant role of body language in shaping leadership perception.

Have you noticed that a person who makes eye contact, uses warm facial expressions, and displays open body language conveys a sense of support, trust, and collaboration? Conversely, have you noticed that a person with slumped shoulders, collapsed chest, and cast-down eyes who is walking lethargically is not someone you are likely to rate as having leadership qualities or being someone you would trust? What about a person who struts with their chest puffed up and has their nose in the air as if they decided they are better than everyone else? These three examples, respectively, suggest body language that is confident, withdrawn, and arrogant. Body language may signal to other people what you might be feeling inside, and more importantly, also tells your brain what emotions to experience.

Try this experiment: Slump your shoulders, collapse your chest, look down at the ground, and try to convince yourself that you feel great, energized, excited, and ready to go! Most people find it hard to reconcile the discrepancies that occur when the body tells the brain one thing but self-talk tells the brain something else. Cognitive science labels this phenomenon "cognitive dissonance." Cognitive dissonance results from the feeling of discomfort that arises when your behaviors don't align with your beliefs.

Now, try this experiment and see what it feels like: Sit up tall, being alert without stiffness or tension; set your chin parallel to the ground; bring your shoulders back without sticking out your chest; and relax your jaw and eyebrows. Now, tell yourself how sad, depressed, and unwell you are, and try to convince yourself of these feelings while remaining in this posture. How did you do? Did you experience cognitive dissonance?

You can change your mind by changing your body language. The use of power poses, when they are held for two minutes with conviction, has been shown to increase confidence, boost mood, stimulate feelings of power, and improve performance. Examples of power poses include:

- confident boss (placing the hands behind the head and putting the feet up on a desk)

- superhero pose (standing with feet hip distance apart and placing the hands on the hips like Superman or Wonder Woman)
- victory pose (lifting the arms in the air in a "v" shape as if you just won something).

Amy Cuddy, a researcher at Harvard, is best known for her work with power poses, although her work has been controversial, as it's been suggested that her hormonal changes and risk-taking data related to power poses may have been inflated or exaggerated.[49] Cuddy still claims that her work with power poses leads to more confidence, physiological changes, and risk-taking behavior when participants hold one of the three aforementioned power poses for two minutes. I encourage you to experiment with using power poses and take control of your body language to lift your mood and feel more open and confident, which will help convince your brain that you feel more confident. Using the breath for performance techniques stacked with confident body language has shifted how many of my athletes feel prior to their performances. Test it for yourself prior to training. Relax away any negative, anxious, or uptight body language by shifting into more confident, powerful body posture and constructive self-talk, and breathing for performance to give yourself a competitive advantage.

## Setting Goals and Intentions for Deliberate Practice

Deliberate practice is the key to accelerating your progress toward attaining your goals and aligning with your desired identities. Many athletes go through the motions of practice without having a clear connection between their efforts and their performance, which leads to slow and frustrating progress. Mindless repetition with a focus on quantity without attention to quality tends to lead to overuse injuries, lack of improvement, and lackluster performance.

I worked with a collegiate baseball player who used to do rep after rep, constantly trying to fix his swing. He was over-efforting in his upper body and hence began to develop shoulder pain. The combination of overthinking and over-repping on his swing resulted in detriments to his performance, lacking trust in his abilities, and having no measurable improvement. More reps are not necessarily better, especially since this athlete was heading toward overuse injury, overthinking, over-efforting, and not improving the trust in his swing. Every hitter knows that too many swing thoughts do not improve performance.

In contrast, deliberate, focused, high-quality practice doing fewer reps and aiming at incremental improvements can lead to significant and consistent gains, making the connection between practice and performance more tangible.

When he focused on quality over quantity, his practice subsequently became more deliberate, allowing this incredible baseball player to quiet his mind and focus on quality reps and on his intention for batting practice while reducing overthinking and the potential for injury. He changed from doing 100 hits to doing four sets of four quality hits, paying attention to each hit and learning from them. In the batter's box, he remembered what worked when he ran his routine, keeping his thoughts simple so he could time bat to ball, hit home runs, and set school records. By the end of our two years of working together, he set new personal bests two years in a row, enjoyed the sport more, reversed his depression and anxiety, set university records for home runs in a season along with other offensive stats, became a leader of his team, and was nominated for a Buster Posey Award for being the nation's top DI collegiate catcher. These changes were not just due to only discussing deliberate practice for two years! It was doing his intentional practice that instigated building trust in himself and his swing.

Deliberate practice requires reflecting on what you need to work on to own your confidence and skills. A precise, non-shame-based examination of your areas of improvement will help you design a plan to break down these skills into smaller areas to work on intentionally during practice. Practice becomes much more interesting, fun, and engaging when you work on improving smaller parts of your game. Trying to work on everything at once or doing absent-minded reps makes practices less satisfying and more draining. Instead, make practice more interesting by setting intentional mini-process goals that build confidence to improve your game. Even the pros often break a skill down to its tiniest components to maintain mastery over the fundamentals. Make your process goals so small that you cannot fail to build your confidence over time.

Work on deliberately building quality reps to practice your technique and form, then add accuracy, consistency, and speed of execution, as well as pressure to make fast, accurate decisions. Sometimes, you must practice slower to gain quality and accuracy before adding intensity, pressure, and speed. Finally, put it all together so that your speed, quality, consistency, and accuracy of execution under pressure are at game speed. Variability of drill intensity balanced with rest and recovery, mental training, and supportive, direct feedback accelerates the learning process and keeps practices fun and engaging. Once you consistently execute under high pressure with high accuracy and quality, deliberately practice other skills and tactical situations. The best performers in the world know there are always areas for improvement. They challenge themselves on how accurately and consistently they can execute under pressure during practice, so they can own their skills and decision-making in competition. They imagine themselves in adverse situations and envision how they will problem-solve to handle them. Competition can become relatively easy and fun as it may start to feel like a reprieve from the intense, deliberate and challenging practice sessions!

What skills and tactical situations do you need to practice deliberately? How can you break the skills and decision-making process down to something so small that you cannot fail, and then over time add speed, accuracy, pressure, and consistency to your mix? Can you successfully perform your skills nine times out of 10 regardless of the pressure, intensity, or imaginary opponents? Deliberate, quality practice grows your confidence on the road to owning it!

## Mental Rehearsal and Mental Reps

Doing mental reps allows you to preserve your body physically while still practicing and preparing for excellent performances. Mental rehearsal or the use of imagery is one of the most important skills an athlete can develop. Some athletes are more kinesthetic when they practice their game mentally, feeling the experience instead of seeing their performance in their mind's eye, while others are more auditory and predominantly hear their performances. Most athletes can visualize a movie or highlight reel in their mind's eye, and practicing this skill helps your brain create or repeat an outstanding performance by strengthening the neuronal connections for how you want to perform. What wires together, fires together!

Mental rehearsal is not just for athletes. Parents, coaches, and TAT members can use mental rehearsal to see themselves perform successfully in their roles, responding with composure and confidence, to contribute to positive sporting experiences and a winning culture.

Mental rehearsal can be part of a pre-performance routine and/or a post-performance learning or review process. Mental rehearsal and visualization are different skills, although the two are often confused. Visualization may use similar brain mechanisms as mental rehearsal, but the eyes are open and the technique is used for a brief period of time (one to three seconds). It should be used during your performance to see the action just before you take the action. For example, a golfer might visualize the trajectory of the ball and how and where it lands and rolls just before taking the shot. A free throw shooter in basketball might stare at the back of the rim and hear the swoosh of the net before taking the shot. Before a direct kick in soccer, the player might visualize the ball's path going into the top right corner of the goal just before taking the shot. It is the same with a serve in tennis, a throw-in in soccer, or other set plays: The athlete trusts the body to know how to do what the brain just visualized. Pairing specific visualizations with powerful words can help focus the brain, such as saying "spot on," "bang it," or "long and smooth" while visualizing specifically what you want to happen just before taking action. Relax and trust your body and brain to know how to make the play.

Imagery or mental rehearsal is like playing a master reel of your highlights in your mind's eye or feeling the reality in your body. An imagery session may last from five to 20 minutes. You can also focus on how you wish to play in the upcoming competition by seeing and feeling yourself reaching your goal. Ski racers often mentally rehearse their race to the exact time they aim to achieve. The more vivid, clear, and believable the whole-body experience is, the better the brain builds the neuronal connections to live the experience in real life. According to research studies using fMRI tests, your brain activates similarly during real and imagined events, meaning that the same areas of the brain light up when you perform the task as when you imagine it.[50] This provides good evidence that you are gaining from mental reps without always needing to do the physical work.

Use these four imagery or mental rehearsal types:

- Mastery
  o involves seeing yourself perform similarly to when you've been at your best or how you want to perform in the future
  o may include seeing yourself mimicking the things that your favorite role models, heroes, and heroines do
  o may include seeing yourself in control and mastering situations in competition like a pro

- Corrective imagery
  - allows you to practice in your mind's eye what you want to do, not what you don't want to do
  - involves seeing yourself correct your mistakes as opposed to playing a mistake over and over again in your mind's eye or watching a mistake over and over again on video
  - requires training, practice, and discipline to not beat yourself for a mistake
  - any athlete who gets caught up in mentally replaying their mistakes is essentially practicing what they don't want, which reinforces neuronal pathways in the wrong direction; you would never physically practice mistakes, so athletes should stop practicing them mentally
- Adversity imagery
  - involves seeing yourself handling challenges and high pressure with composure and confidence
  - allows for practicing positive responses to adverse situations in mental rehearsal and prepares you for responding well to the inevitable mistakes that you or others will make
  - lets you see yourself capitalizing on mistakes, staying focused, and maintaining your confidence instead of shrinking back and losing confidence
- Healing and recovery mental rehearsal
  - involves seeing yourself return to the sport feeling stronger after an injury, with greater clarity and passion, and a healed, fit, and ready mind, heart, and body
  - is an affirmation that your body, mind, and emotions know how to heal, that you are recovering well, and that you are getting stronger
  - may help athletes recover faster, move through rehab with greater well-being, and return to playing more confidently
  - can be a post-performance routine that you can use to recover well and return to training feeling strong and energized

If you have difficulty seeing yourself perform in your mind's eye, you can watch videos of your favorite athletes or role models you admire and then imagine yourself doing the same actions. For example, if you are a goalkeeper, compile videos of great saves and plays. For other athletes, compile highlight videos of favorite goals, baskets, races, or impressive moments to prepare you mentally for practice, training, or competition. Your brain should compute what you want your body to create as you train your neuropathways to make automatic decisions. Use imagery as part of your alter-ego transformation ritual toward becoming more like your athlete's choice identity. Remember to also have a post-performance mental routine to bring yourself back down from your alter ego into your relationship identity so you keep your beastly competitive side on the field, court, pool, or pitch. Mental rehearsal is not just for big games, it's an everyday practice, like a physical warm-up. Keep your routines the same regardless of how big or small the competition is to prepare yourself consistently and reduce feelings of overwhelm or overthinking when the big games arrive.

During the years I was training, I practiced playing in the Olympics thousands of times in my head. At the actual Olympic Games, when the coach told me at halftime that I was going in the second half and to get warmed up, I felt ready. Though I had never played in front of 25,000 fans chanting "USA! USA!" and certainly not in my hometown of Atlanta, nor played at the Olympics, I told myself, "I have played thousands of times physically and mentally, so I am ready to solve whatever problems arise." I stepped into the second half of the game against Australia, the number one team in the world and most dominant field hockey team the world had ever seen, already down by four goals, I had my gold medal moment by doing what I could do to contribute to the team's success. As a goalkeeper, during my half, I shut out the number one team in the world (who were eventual Olympic gold medal winners in 1996). My goalkeeper coach, Michele Madison, told me after the game that she was nervous watching me warm up because I looked so calm. I was calm because I had been there so many times in my mind's eye, even though it was nothing I had ever done before in real life.

Use imagery techniques before practice sessions so your routine is specific and tailored for you based on what helps you play well regardless of the opponents or the challenges of the moment. Mental rehearsal is one of the most powerful tools in the mental skills toolbox. Find a way to use imagery to transform your game and be ready for your gold-medal moments.

# Gratitude

Gratitude is not just a feeling, it's a powerful catalyst for personal growth. It's impossible to feel both grateful and depressed or anxious simultaneously. When we appreciate the gifts, challenges, and opportunities we have, we develop a skill that helps us navigate life's 10,000 tears and 10,000 sorrows. Without gratitude, we will struggle needlessly. It is a potent tool for mental health, helping us accept and appreciate what is, and reminds us that the universe is for us and not against us. Maintaining gratitude keeps us open to unseen lessons and opportunities, which can significantly improve our mental well-being.

Gratitude is also a powerful tool for enhancing our relationships. Focusing on what we appreciate in others allows us to let go of disappointments, resentments, and regrets. Cultivating gratitude helps us be more optimistic and resilient, and physically, mentally, and emotionally healthier for working through inevitable challenges. It's a reminder that we are not alone on this adventure, and there are people, disguised and obvious, around us who contribute to our growth and well-being. When you look back on the challenges you overcame with appreciation for who you have become today, can you feel gratitude for all you have learned? It may be difficult at times to feel thankful, and we do not often appreciate a challenge while we are going through it, but we can practice slowing down to recognize the gift we're being given as quickly as possible.

Optimizing our potential and reaching what we can achieve requires experiencing challenges, setbacks, and disappointments. These are not roadblocks but rather can be viewed as stepping stones to growth. If the goal was too easy and you achieved it right away, then you likely did not set a challenging enough goal and you had far more in your tank than you gave yourself credit for. Too many people unwittingly set low-level, mediocre goals for themselves because of their anticipated fear of experiencing failure, shame, and embarrassment if they don't achieve them. However, embracing challenges and setbacks as being opportunities for growth is the key to unlocking what you are truly capable of, and reminding yourself that you have not achieved the goal...yet.

The root of the word "mediocrity" means, "to be stuck in the middle of the mountain." One of my biggest drivers for working toward big dreams and goals was the fear of being mediocre or average. However, I've made peace with the fact that there are plenty of things at which I am still average. You will always find people who are better and worse than you at any number of skills. Comparing yourself to your previous self and focusing on being grateful for the potential to continue to improve is the growth mindset that allows you to progress and enjoy the process of improving. Instead of constantly looking at how far you need to go, remember to celebrate how far you've come!

Gratitude, when combined with reflection, becomes a powerful tool for learning. Reflecting on what went well and what needs work helps you learn productively. Optimism, hope, and confidence help you appreciate and acknowledge the good and stay resilient during challenges. As part of a post-performance routine, writing down the parts of the performance for which you are grateful can be a reminder that you can do hard things and that you get to do them, which is a privilege. Starting with gratitude can give you the courage to address what you did well and what you will improve for next time. Consider how you will design deliberate practices to address your areas of improvement or use the scientifically validated goal-setting WOOP method by Dr. Oettingen.

Other gratitude practices can include writing in a journal dedicated to gratitude. Some people use a gratitude jar into which they or their partner, family members, colleagues, coaching staff, and/or teammates put slips of colorful paper with written messages of gratitude. You can then reach into the jar during challenging times to be reminded of the good stuff. Other practices include writing a gratitude letter to someone who has played an essential role in your life or impacted you positively. You might just feel equally as good as the person who gets to receive your letter.

Regardless of what method you choose, you will want to turn to gratitude throughout the day. The comedian, podcaster, and writer Neal Brennan, on his podcast called Blocks,[51] talks about gratitude as a practice he intentionally builds into his day five times, similar to the way that Muslims turn toward Mecca five times a day. Without it, he describes that his mind has a tendency to turn dark, and he starts to feel depressed and anxious. Having a mental checklist of things that you are grateful for can help. Finally, slowing down to thank and appreciate someone and letting them know what they mean to you is one of the greatest gifts that can be given. Include yourself as being someone to thank too, and express gratitude to your future self for inspiring you to excellence.

# Chapter 15

# The Four Phases of Performance

The four phases of performance are preparation, pre-performance (including priming), during performance (focusing), and post-performance (recovery and learning for growth). A performance matrix provides a structured view of the four performance phases and how to approach your game through training, mental preparation, sleep, fueling and hydrating, competition, and recovery. From there, you can create a plan to address and consistently attend to the four phases to maximize your performance, health, and goal achievement over a sustainable period of time (see the performance matrix plan in Appendix B).

## Preparation Phase

Preparation is the culmination of all the work and learning that has taken place from the inception of your playing your sport or endeavor to the week before a competition or an important event. Some practitioners or researchers call the year-long periodization of training the "preparation phase," which certainly makes sense, but I take a far longer view that all components that have influenced the development of the athlete or performer to date are in the preparation phase because it encompasses all the learning of what to do and not to do. This phase is a testament to your dedication and hard work, and it's where the seeds of success are sown.

Preparation entails all the training, practices, skill development, team meetings, film review, nutrition, sleep, body care, mental-emotional-relational development, and prior competitions that have prepared the performer to be the healthiest, most optimized version of themselves for an upcoming competition or event. With sufficient preparation, the mind, body, emotions, and spirit can be ready technically, tactically, and strategically to be at their best for "show-time."

While preparing, using simple, consistent routines that put you into an optimal performance state is ideal, such as playing music to help you feel either more energized or calm. I encourage you to have specific repeatable routines for priming your mind, body and emotions and to have a backup plan in case your transportation arrives late to the competition and your priming time is shortened. I caution you not to rely on an overly specific routine that will hinder you if you do not do it just right. Conversely, being too casual and just hoping for the best is not an optimal pre-performance routine either. Hope is not a strategy, but solid preparation is.

## Prepare for the unexpected

Buck Brannaman, the Horse Whisperer, is arguably one of the finest horse trainers of modern times. He was highly involved in the 1998 movie *The Horse Whisperer*, which demonstrates the skillful and compassionate means of a cowboy who could connect with horses, soothe their angst, and train people to respond effectively to horses. As a horse lover who wanted to improve my equestrian skills, I learned at the start of my training that horses can be dangerous. Things can go wrong quickly if you don't respect the horses and understand how they think and behave.

During the Buck Brannaman clinics I attended with my two horses when I was a complete novice, he repeatedly reminded the participants to "prepare for the unexpected." In his charismatic but direct way, he taught that a great horseman has a certain "feel." To me, this meant gaining experience in various scenarios and with a variety of horses, spending hours in the saddle and on the ground, figuring it out, reflecting, seeing what worked, seeking feedback and opinions from others, trying again, failing, getting back up again, and trying new things. Developing the "feel" timing and intuition comes from experience and paying attention. Buck was curious whether or not students could learn the sense of having this "feel" or timing or whether some were just born with it. I believe that students can improve their "feel" with practice, coaching, and repetition, and that having some level of innate athleticism and coachability also helps.

Buck learned during the clinics that I was a psychologist, and one day he asked me, "I just wanna know how you teach others 'feel.' How do you teach 'feel'?" Unbeknownst to me, he was not actually interested in any answers or in my thoughts on the topic, but rather it seemed that he was asking rhetorically to encourage me to ponder how I would improve my "feel" as a beginner horse whispering enthusiast. Very astute of him. My thoughts on "feel" are that developing it takes years of experience in a variety of circumstances and with a variety of horses, with an experienced instructor who is patient enough to offer corrections on timing. Some riders and trainers will be quicker than others if they are more athletic, open to coaching, and willing to put in the practice, which is the same road most novices need to take to master the "feel" for any skill. Feel will also help you be prepared for and anticipate the unexpected.

## Pre-Performance Phase

Although some athletes and coaches make the mistake of only preparing the night before or on the day of the competition and expecting to perform well, the pre-performance phase starts the week before a competition or significant event. This phase consists of implementing and practicing the corresponding specific game plan, and the consistent pre-performance routines to prime the mind, body, emotions, and spirit just before competition to confidently execute at the highest level possible.

Coaches typically offer specific strategies and tactics pertaining to the next competition for the athlete to implement in the upcoming training and practices. Depending on the sport and the coaching staff's philosophy, coaches will often set up video reviews of the tendencies of the opponent, review key players, and discuss the strategies for attacking and defending against those patterns. Practice and training schedules will be periodized so athletes can, hopefully, feel well-rested and optimally prepared to give their full effort toward whatever it takes during competition.

Having good-quality sleep, adequate nutrition with performance and recovery foods, proper hydration, overall body care, and optimal mental performance are not just key factors leading up to the competition but should also be included in daily routines and habits. High-quality deliberate practices and training with a focus on improvement and tightening the execution specific to the competition should be added while refining what the athlete or team does best to make for a winning formula. The aim is to fill the athlete's tank prior to competition so they can give whatever energy is required for a great performance. Depending on the timing of the competition within a season, all might not need to be given especially if another competition is around the corner. In those cases, be efficient and give what is needed to ensure a win.

As preparation funnels down to competition day, specific pre-competition or priming routines often start the night before with mental rehearsal, pre-competition meals and hydration plans, and relaxing and resting. On the day of the competition, depending on the timing of the bout, teams or athletes might do a light walkthrough or team walk several hours prior. Specific physical, mental, and skill warm-ups may be done to prime the body and mind for optimal arousal states, igniting the confidence, focus, and readiness to perform. Most teams have specific warm-ups that they do to prepare for optimal performance, such as doing mobility exercises and dynamic movement patterns, practicing skill execution, getting the heart rate up for brief bursts of 90 percent effort to improve blood flow and lung capacity, and dynamic small-team tactics to get the offense and defense primed and flowing for the competition. Every athlete has a unique approach to their mental and physical preparation. Individual and collective priming activities help each athlete to prepare for their personal and collective best performances.

## Know your number

Knowing your number pertains to understanding your optimal energy state, or the level of mental and physical activation and alertness needed to perform at your best. Think of a recent time when you competed or performed really well or were even at your best. Now, rate your arousal state during that event on a 10-point, with 1 being completely relaxed and 10 being the most intense, beating your chest with rebel yells. Where did your optimal energy state fall on that relaxed to hyped scale?

My optimal energy state during competition needed to be at around a 6, meaning I was excited and energized enough to show up with the strong intent to play well. I tended to be an anxious athlete, so I needed to be more on the calm, confident, clear-headed side of arousal and focus on trusting myself and remembering that I was prepared. In contrast, an athlete like Ray Lewis, former linebacker for the Baltimore Ravens, was probably at a 12 in his optimal energy state! He was known for the show he put on prior to playing, which got his team and fans riled up. Tennis phenom Roger Federer, on the other hand, often looked as calm as a Zen master and perhaps his number was closer to a 3 or 4.

## What coaches can do

The coaching staff's job is to prepare the team or athlete(s) well to tactically and strategically execute the specific skills to beat the tendencies of the competition. Balancing training, practices, film reviews, team meetings, travel itineraries, and individual connection and encouragement with each team member are all part of the responsibilities of coaches during the run-up phase to competition.

The team may have a dinner or meeting the night before the competition to review what the foci of practices and development are for getting ready. This discussion may include reminders of the strategies, assignments against certain key players and competitors and their tendencies, and the overall game plan so athletes feel ready to mentally rehearse their role and the game plan on their own. The gathering might also include some bonding activities to leave the team members feeling good about each other, increase trust and flow, and be in sync.

Some coaches have the players dress formally prior to a game as a symbol of treating the game professionally when traveling to a competition site. Remind players about what is in their control so they can go to bed feeling confident, clear-minded, hydrated, and fueled, and get a good-quality eight hours of sleep. The day of prep may also include a team meal, morning walkthrough, or team walk for loosening up and connecting, all of which are dependent on the time of the competition.

## What parents/guardians and support people can do

Depending on the level of competition, the levels of involvement from family, friends, or partners will vary. From driving the athlete to the competition, helping to prepare snacks and hydration bottles, reviewing what gear is needed, and helping to pack bags or equipment, the job of family of friends is to play an encouraging support role. Optimally, ask how you can be helpful, if there's anything the athlete needs, and let them know that you'll be cheering for them and the team. Letting the athlete know that you love to watch them play may help them relax by reminding them that they should focus on enjoying playing the sport without unnecessary pressure.

The support team of the athlete must not become a distraction, as some support people have self-serving tactics that detract from the athlete's performance, such as turning the spotlight on themselves, instigating drama, and stirring up unnecessary conflict. Letting your own nerves become the point of focus is not helpful to playing your role well. Your role is to support and encourage, but that does not mean being treated disrespectfully, being submissive or servile, or fussing over the athlete.

## What TAT members can do pre-performance

TAT members all play a role in athlete and team readiness. The athletic trainer(s) will provide athletes with pre-existing conditions pre-hab treatment, taping, and stretching, but not all athletes will see the trainer. Athletes may go to the training room to complete their own protocol. Trainers and/or team dietitians will get the hydration bottles and fueling station ready unless the athletes have their own, or the parents are involved in preparing snacks for game day.

Depending on the temperature of the day, ATCs or dietitians may have salt tablets or anti-cramping solutions ready to be administered. S&C coaches often take athletes through their mobility and physical priming routines, unless they are player- or coach-led. Mental performance coaches might lead the team the night before or 90 minutes prior to the competition through a relaxation, mental imagery, or meditation routine. The presence of the TAT members is a reminder to the athlete of what the team has been working on in the various performance domains and offers support and encouragement to the athletes. In university or high school settings, some TAT members may have several teams with whom they are working, so they will not be able to attend every competition of all of their teams.

## During-Performance Phase

The during-performance phase starts when the competition begins and ends when the event is over. During performance includes any time-outs, stoppage of plays, or halftime or quarter-time breaks. This phase is about staying focused on competition tasks and execution; maintaining a sense of joy, freedom, and effortless effort; responding to one's own errors and those of others without stress or panic; communicating with coaches and teammates; keeping well fueled; hydrating; and maintaining a sense of confidence no matter what.

At the start of your during-performance phase, you can go into your event or competition with the confidence that you have prepared well and can trust your training. Your job is to focus on your game plan, use your signature strengths, and stay connected to your teammates with effective, uplifting, and tactical communication. Give your best effort for yourself, your teammates, your coaches, the game, your parents, friends, family, and the fans. The more fun you can have and the more effortless effort you give in the moment without overthinking, the more likely it is that you will compete hard and well.

Performance is complex, but complexity is what makes competition interesting, engaging, challenging, and fun. Performing well requires optimal thinking, great timing, learning, effort, and memory, as competition tests our grit, skills, preparation, strategies, teamwork, and communication. Getting to perform is why we do all the hard work to prepare, and we then get to see what's working and not working well. Figuring out how to bring it all together at the right time to maintain a high level of performance throughout the competition keeps us returning to the sport. Seeking the flow and feelings of performance excellence feels good. The paradox of performance involves keeping your thoughts simple so the body can do the complex actions for which you have trained. Strong footwork and bodywork set the stage for natural execution, but the secret sauce of high performance that binds a team together is trust. When everyone on the team is following the self-mastery plan, trust has the best chance of being developed.

And don't forget other secret tips like positive self-talk, body language, and communication to keep the team or athlete focused. Using power words or statements for mistake recovery, such as "what's next," "turn the page," "next play," or "WIN" (an acronym for "what's important now") can help with refocusing on the task. Hanging your head or shoulders after a mistake communicates to others that you are focused on the error and are not in the present moment, which won't help you fix the error. There is no escaping making mistakes in sports. How teams and athletes respond to their own mistakes and those of teammates, opponents, referees, judges or umpires, coaches, spectators, or parents can impact the momentum and outcome of the competition. Those who capitalize on moving forward from mistakes instead of shrinking from them tend to win.

Many of the athletes I work with came to me because they tended to train and perform well during practice but may have had difficulty performing during competition. This is called performance anxiety, whereby they did not trust themselves to perform the way they are capable of performing. I have offered plenty of strategies here to bring your 'A game' regardless of the opponents, which is why I recommend that you train for and practice all elements of performance. Training for adversity or worst-case scenarios prepares you mentally, physically, and emotionally for more challenging conditions. No one knows what the outcome of the competition will be until the game is played. I believe that anyone can win on any given day, even when the odds are stacked against an individual or team. So play hard to the best of your ability, regardless of the opponent.

Develop team and individual strategies to maintain momentum using pre-commitments and algorithms such as "if-then" statements. Overthinking tends to be problematic for any athlete, but algorithms can help with keeping one's thoughts focused on the right actions. An example of a helpful "if-then" statement might be: "If we are down, then stay aggressive and compete fiercely. Giving up is never an option."

Player leaders or coaches may make a call to use possession strategies for managing the clock and slowing things down. When an athlete is fatigued, it is easy for them to start getting sloppy, particularly at the end of the game. No matter the sport, finishing strong is what champions do, and they train well so they can finish strong. Remaining poised, maintaining an aggressive attitude, and not giving up builds pride and stamina for the next competition. When the momentum shifts, knowing how to regain control is an important strategy to practice with key player leaders. During-performance strategies include knowing when to slow things down and when to turn on the pressure and put the hammer down. "If-then" statements and pre-commitments help athletes manage and learn to control the flow of performance without overthinking.

## *What coaches can do during performance*

Coaching staff must be mindful of controlling their verbal and nonverbal body language. Choosing words wisely, knowing when to coach or let the athlete figure it out, keeping their heads and chests up, and using long, controlled exhales to stay in the present moment will help coaches with their decision-making and communication. Usually, an athlete knows when they've made a mistake and is already feeling bad about it, and coaches yelling at athletes from the sideline about what they did wrong doesn't tend to help.

Don't use "don't." Tell athletes what you want, not what you don't want. Another pet peeve of mine is when coaches yell out to athletes negatively, "What were you thinking?" while the athletes are still playing. Athletes need to focus on what's next rather than thinking about their mistakes. Pulling an athlete immediately after a mistake is a sure way to chip away at their confidence and result in them playing scared and looking to the coaches on the sidelines for reassurance. Trust the athlete to figure it out and let their teammates help them. Communicate to the team during practices that you expect them to work through mistakes. If they still continue to make the same mistakes, then coaches can step in and play their role of being educators rather than punishers.

If it's a team sport, rotate athletes so they can play fresh and give it their all when they are in. Maintaining the momentum of the game and encouraging coaches to listen to their gut instincts is important, but coaches who base their decisions on scientific evidence (such as when an athlete reaches a certain level of load or exertion) rather than on their emotions, favorites, prejudices, or biases tend to have more success in competition because team members will have more trust in the system. Of course, the coaching staff must also trust players' maturity, fitness, skills, and knowledge to institute such an approach. All athletes must learn to play well together, no matter who is in the lineup, and that is handled in the preparation phase.

We have all witnessed coaches losing their minds on the sidelines. I appreciate passion and intense competitiveness, and coaches should question lousy calls and ask for the right one. However, since they are the primary leaders and decision-makers, coaches need to be in control of themselves. Undoubtedly, the coach plays an important leadership role.

You may recall that the acronym SEED stands for supporter, exemplar, educator, and decision-maker, which are the roles and responsibilities of the coach. Depending on the sport, the coach may be highly involved in calling plays or trusting the athletes to make the calls. A coaching staff who has prepared the athletes well can relax and trust the performance to unfold. Staying focused, clear-headed, and calm helps athletes, especially younger ones, focus on doing their jobs.

## What parents can do during performance

The roles and responsibilities of parents are summarized by the acronym STEP, which as a reminder stands for supporter, encourager, and embracer of challenges; teacher and disciplinarian; exemplar; and giver of presence. Being respectful rather than critical, supporting other athletes on the team besides just your child, managing your own emotions, and not getting overly involved are all ways that a parent can maintain perspective and support and encourage athletes' enjoyment of the competition. Controlling your attitude, body language, and words and not trying to control others are the best ways to contribute to a winning system. Your own self-mastery is a great place to start.

## What TATs can do during performance

Athletic trainers and dietitians will likely help with maintaining athletes' hydration. Of course, the ATC will be available to help any athlete with taping or attending to an acute injury. Mental performance coaches might remind players of performance cues, assignments, signature strengths, or strategies and help athletes manage their arousal levels. At more advanced levels, S&C coaches and/or ATCs might be responsible for reviewing real-time load data and advising the coaching staff on substitution recommendations based on load.

## Post-Performance Phase

The post-performance phase starts immediately after the competition is over and includes all recovery tactics for the mind, body, emotions, and spirit to refill athletes' proverbial tanks before starting the preparation and pre-performance phase again. Fueling; hydration; cooldowns; using therapeutic modalities such as rolling, stretching, attending to minor injuries, and ice baths as prescribed; sleep; film review; reflection; and evaluation are all related to recovery. Physical recovery practices help repair and strengthen your muscles instead of them being in a constant state of breaking down. Once you have completed your post-performance review, taken notes in your performance journal, and have a concrete, simple plan for how you will work on making improvements, it's important to take time to get some rest.

But recovery isn't just physical—it's also mental and reflective: looking at what you learned, which includes not just what you need to fix but also what you did well so you can train your brain on what you want to repeat. Learning is one of the essential and often undervalued phases of performance. Without reflecting objectively on what worked, what needs work, and how you will improve, lessons that could've been learned will likely return at inopportune times when the stakes are higher. If you can learn early and often by reflecting without judgment or attachment and then implement the changes, you will surpass your opponents who are unwilling or afraid or embarrassed to address their mistakes. Rather than beating yourself up for missteps, embrace and learn from them to achieve exponential growth. Celebrating your small wins and moments of success builds your wall of confidence.

Post-performance rituals, routines, and actions often include shaking hands with your opponents; thanking referees, judges, umpires, organizers, and coaching staff; engaging in a proper cooldown; having a team huddle with coaches for key reflections from staff and teammates; attending to fueling and hydration needs within the first 30–60 minutes after the competition ends; and then being released to the media, friends, and family.

I inform my athletes that the "money" is in the post-performance routines. From my experience as a practitioner and coach, most athletes regularly attend practice and training sessions during the preparation phase, but a smaller percentage of those athletes have consistent mental pre-performance routines (PPRs), an even smaller percentage have specific mental during-performance routines (DPRs), and the smallest percentage of athletes have consistent post-performance routines that include a mental component. Those who maintain an effective post-performance mental routine that consists of more than just a few stretches, a bit of hydration and fueling, and a few words from the coaches can be optimally prepared for the next practice or competition. Structured routines provide a sense of organization and control, helping you optimize your performance and reach your goals.

Regardless of the outcome of a competition—a glorious win, a disastrous loss, or a semi-reasonable tie—it's crucial to incorporate mental skills into your post-performance routines. Objective, open, and curious reflections are key to identifying the lessons needed for personal growth.

While there's no specific research on the percentage of athletes who actively engage in these four phases with intent and focus, it's generally observed that pro- and elite-level athletes are more likely to consistently engage in all four phases, placing value on each phase without short-changing any of them.

In my own work with high-level performers, I've seen how difficult it is to maintain discipline across all four phases, which is why they seek professional support. It takes an incredible amount of discipline to remain consistent, and that's why the GOATs perform at such high levels: They have professionals like me around them to help them be consistent. Receiving professional support is not a sign of weakness, but a testament to your commitment to excellence in maintaining discipline and consistency in your routines. My clients and I work together to refine and consistently execute their routines in the pre-, during-, and post-phases of performance so that their overall preparation for any opponent is timed to be on target. When athletes are consistent with their routines, they can learn from their mistakes and understand what's working and what's not. Rarely, if ever, is a perfect competition ever executed, and there is usually room for improvement.

Consider including a film review of your favorite plays, whether you were in them or not, as part of your highlight reel. Notice your mistakes and consider how you plan to correct them, using mental rehearsal to visualize yourself making improvements rather than perseverating on the error. Film review of oneself or the team can be a great learning tool for seeing yourself do more of what you want and for correcting the mistakes in positioning, timing, mental or physical effort, decisions, or technique.

The only way to learn is through long-term trial and error to determine what will work best for you. No one on the planet has grown in their self-mastery and become great without going through years of facing challenges, making mistakes, learning hard lessons, and experiencing repeated failures and disappointments. Of course, the joy of victory helps maintain the commitment to pursuing excellence. The performer persists because they are dedicated to seeing their goals come to fruition. Talk to any self-master, and you will find someone who has not had an easy road to their success. The bricks of wins, successes, disappointments, losses, victories, and tribulations all paved the road to self-mastery.

To support your ongoing adventure toward mastery, I recommend incorporating specific mental reflection processes during the post-performance phase. You can try one at a time for two weeks or alternate every other day with using one on even days and a different one on odd days, using modifications as needed. These processes are structured in a specific order, and each method takes a brief three to eight minutes. Once you become more comfortable, you may reduce your time to just one to three minutes. Make the process meaningful for you, which connects memory to learning and makes you more apt to remember to take action with intention. Unless there's an action taken from what we have learned that results in making changes, no authentic learning has actually taken place. As Maya Angelou reminds us, "Do the best you can until you know better. Then when you know better, do better."

## Well-Better-How

I learned this reflection method when I was the head of mental conditioning at IMG Academy. The department members and I used this approach consistently to supervise the summer staff in improving their learning and work, and when evaluating a program, event, process, or even a single mental conditioning session or activity. We also asked other people to use the process with us to help improve the programming we delivered.

The Well-Better-How (WBH) method starts by asking, "What went well?" and identifying at least three things that did. We need to intentionally ask this, as we are prone to be negative. Barbara Fredrickson, a prominent researcher in the field of positive psychology, studied the negativity bias and described it as being for survival and safety purposes an inherent human tendency to look for what's wrong, dangerous, and threatening in our environments. According to Fredrickson, thinking about what went well "broadens and builds" the brain's capacity for creativity, possibility, and connection while building personal resources for overall well-being.[52] Your solutions will be more creative when you use this approach than when you beat yourself up for the mistakes you made or if you try to work on everything all at once. Scolding and berating yourself out loud or internally trains your brain in the wrong direction.

Is there an ideal ratio of being realistic or "critical" to being positive that helps you flourish rather than languish? Fredrickson and Marcial Losada suggested in 2005 that the ratio is three positives for every one negative to optimally reinforce the good things, increase well-being and resilience, and advance creative solutions for what we will do better next time.[53] Unfortunately, according to Nick Brown, Alan Sokal, and Harris Friedman in their rebuttal published in 2013, this critical-positivity ratio has largely been debunked for mathematical errors.[54] Though a 3:1 ratio may not be a scientifically validated ratio of positives to negatives, there is a practical value in focusing on what went well without hyper-focusing on what went wrong.

Naturally, high achievement-oriented people search for opportunities to improve and are more apt to focus on what was wrong with their performance. Perfectionists tend to take what they did well for granted because they expect to be correct 100 percent of the time, and hence, they often feel anxious and depressed when they don't achieve an unrealistic expectation. However, we should focus on rewiring our neuropathways for what we want to repeat or improve. We want to gain mental reps by mentally reviewing what works, reflecting on and replaying the good things, and remembering what went well. Starting with what went well gives us the courage to look at what to improve without shaming, blaming, and complaining.

So focus on at least three things you did well, even if you are tempted to say, "I did nothing well!" That's just not true. Include the tiniest moments you can be proud of and want to repeat. If you are involved in a dynamic team sport, ask yourself, did you make a few good passes? Did you communicate well and encourage a teammate? Did you make an important defensive play? What would a supportive teammate or coach tell you about three things you did well? No matter how small the wins and "wells," celebrate them with the enthusiastic internal exclamation, "That's like me!" The brain loves the dopamine hit of celebrating what you want to have more of so you can reproduce the wins automatically.

Now that you have identified at least three things you did well, consider up to three things that you could do better next time. We all have things we need to improve upon, but many athletes, including myself during my early competitive days, write too long a list of mistakes that interfere with positive progress. You cannot work on everything all at once. Rather, prioritize up to three key areas of improvement that you can work on in your upcoming training and practice sessions. The more specific, manageable, and implementable the improvement mini-goals are, the more likely you will progress in a positive direction. Practice sessions can become more specific with deliberate focus and purpose.

The "how" part of the WBH method refers to how you will improve the skills or decisions you want to make. This is where goal-setting skills come into play: Set two or three specific, manageable, and implementable process and performance goals for your next practice. A vague goal, such as a tennis player practicing serves, is not very helpful. "Practice kick serves for 15 minutes, aiming for 70 percent between the cone and the singles sideline" is a more specific and helpful goal to work toward and for your brain to get behind.

The WBH method encourages you to not waste a great opportunity to learn. Ask yourself what you learned about what helps you play well, and repeat these lessons as part of your intentions, routines, and habits. What did you learn about yourself from playing poorly, and how did you respond to mistakes? Did you notice that you did not prepare as well as you could have? Did you not get a good night's sleep? Did you let distractions get in your way, like spending too much time on your phone? Distractions might also include who was watching you play, your self-judgment, lack of using a mistake management plan, and having a poor nutrition or hydration plan. Being objective, nonjudgmental, and honest with self-compassion about what you can do better next time without beating yourself up will put you on a positive path toward progress and mastering your game.

## The 80/20 rule

Some of the athletes I have worked with were so inclined to the negativity bias that I had them practice the 80/20 rule. This entails focusing on a four-to-one ratio such that the athlete recalls four things they did well and one corrective action they want to take. It's not an opportunity to reinforce the behavior you don't want by repeatedly playing the mistake (s) in your head, but rather the corrective action is mindfully focusing on how you would execute next time. By using the 80/20 rule, these athletes elevated their self-esteem, increased their resilience, elongated their focus during competition, recovered more quickly from mistakes, and even enjoyed playing again.

Imagine what would happen if you meaningfully engaged in this process after every practice and training session: hunting and celebrating the good stuff and implementing an improvement plan with a three-to-one positivity/negativity Losada Ratio or a four-to-one 80/20 Rule. How quickly would your game improve with this type of deliberate attention? Most athletes find this to be a fun, rewarding, and motivating process that is not tedious. If you do find this method to be tedious, however, consider how you approach it. Are you open and curious, or do you feel bad about yourself for making mistakes? If so, the 3-2-1 process might be more up your alley.

## 3-2-1 count (post-performance evaluation)

I learned this simple post-performance review process from Bernie Holliday, the Pittsburgh Pirates' director of learning and mental performance. In baseball, knowing the count is important because it tells players, coaches, and fans what the situation is and informs the pitcher and batter what pitches should be thrown. In this case, knowing the count is a post-performance reflection tool for you to use in reflecting on three ups (what went well), two downs (the two things you need to improve), and one takeaway (the key lesson learned that you can take to your next competition or training session).

The WBH and 3-2-1 processes are effective ways to keep your post-performance review simple and focused. They can keep you from going down the proverbial rabbit hole of blaming, shaming, and complaining about yourself internally, complaining about others, or complaining to others about yourself and others.

## What coaches can do post-performance

Coaches can use the WBH or 3-2-1 methods in their post-game team talk to focus on discussing what to reinforce and what needs improvement. Keeping athletes for more than 10–15 minutes after a game will likely be ineffective; athletes may have a decreased attention span because emotions may be running high, and they may be feeling fatigued and ready to recover. Whether the competition resulted in a win or a loss, athletes must focus on recovering, not listening to a coach overstate what the team or individual athletes should have done.

Waiting to review film 12–24 hours post-game allows time for emotions to calm down so that the coaches and team members can reflect more objectively. The staff can look for great plays for the team to repeat and offer some key areas to correct, being mindful that overwhelming a team with too many corrections leaves them feeling defeated and negative. Ripping the team apart says more about the coach's ego than about the team and their terrible play. Discuss the areas of improvement in the context of the next competition or as a form of education for how the team should play. Keeping a balanced approach to learning and correcting for what you want to see more of will elevate and sustain team members' confidence and progress.

## What parents can do post-performance

Asking your child if they want to talk about the competition is helpful, but parents may need to wait for their child to be ready to talk about it. Parents sometimes launch right into saying what they think, which may suggest their opinions matter more and hinder the child from reflecting on their experience. Giving time and space immediately following the competition can help athletes process their own thoughts first.

When they are ready to engage, you can guide the conversation, depending on their age and level. You can offer praise and encouragement by recognizing your athlete's effort or a favorite play, such as: "You and Jamie seemed to be working well together. You had a great play in the second half with the assist." A parent can acknowledge an improvement, perhaps of a specific skill, such as: "I noticed that your backhand has improved. You seemed more comfortable and confident." If the athlete is feeling disappointed, you can tell them it's okay to feel that way and that you are there to support them regardless of the outcome. Remind them that one competition does not define them, and ask what they learned about themselves or competition, or what the better parts of the competition were that they can replicate during the next one. Instead of generalizing the competition as negative, you can ask what parts were fun or what the highlights were even if it was a disappointing loss. Asking an athlete what would be most helpful when discussing the competition shows them respect and encourages their autonomy.

### What TAT members can do post-performance

There might be S&C coaches available to help cool down the team. Dieticians, if available, can provide fueling and rehydration options and consult on recovery meals. Fueling and rehydration or other essential recovery strategies such as rolling and stretching, post-habbing chronic injuries, or treating minor injuries can be addressed by ATCs. Mental performance coaches might offer support or emotional processing of the game with individual athletes, and may also help with a post-performance review using questions, imagery, or meditation to guide mental recovery and reflection. TAT members support athletes in recovering from competition stress and preparing both physically and mentally for future competitions.

## What is Failure?

I believe in only two types of failures: failure to learn and failure to develop character. The "f" word, whether referring to fear, fear of failure, or evaluating yourself as a failure, is often why athletes work with someone like me. I use perspective-building to work together with my clients on perceiving things differently. Repeating what doesn't work and expecting different results comes from a failure to learn, but if you're consciously making a focused effort to improve, you're on the right track. Athletes spend a lot of time getting frustrated that their development is not happening fast enough, which hinders their progress and makes the sport less fun. Like a freshly planted garden, however, you can't keep digging up the seeds to see if they have grown. You wouldn't yell at a rosebud for not blooming yet— development can't be rushed.

Sports skill development is complex and requires practicing countless reps over time. Successful approximations still constitute progress even if the skill isn't fully developed yet. Patience, curiosity, fun, and openness are all necessary ingredients for improvement. Complex sports skills require many components of coordinated movements and proper technique in order to come together with the right timing. There is a fine line between refining your skill and continuing to micro-adjust to the detriment of not trusting yourself.

Beyond technical skills, character development is essential. If a person is overly self-focused, fails to help other people, has little to no awareness of their impacts on others, and hurts others in their pursuits, the individual's character may be called into question and this situation may be considered to be a failure of character development. Developing quality character is the most important benefit that sports are intended to provide. If an athlete with poor character wins a championship, that person was pursuing the wrong game that only winning matters. If an athlete wins and is miserable inside, the PACT system failed to develop the whole person. Per the expression, "Hurt people hurt people," violence is most often committed by people who have had violence done to them, which is why developing the characters of athletes is so important to me. Empowering athletes, parents, coaches, and TAT practitioners to be their best selves paves the way for healthier communities, and it's a commitment and responsibility that everyone in the PACT system must uphold.

You are playing the right game if you have begun developing self-mastery to own your confidence. If you are learning to maintain a sense of self, joy, and confidence, and are staying connected with others, you have already won and will continue to win in the long run. Winning the inner game of self-mastery leads to winning external games also. The journey of self-mastery is not just about winning on the field, but about winning in life, too. It's about becoming the best versions of yourself, and that's a victory worth striving for.

Only you can ultimately bring out your unique strengths, gifts, and talents. Stop judging yourself so harshly and celebrate your small wins that will turn into bigger wins. Simply correct the areas that need work without shaming, blaming, criticizing, and complaining. Maintaining a balanced approach where you can enjoy and acknowledge your small wins on the way to achieving your WIGs, while also improving what needs work, will keep you motivated in ways that most benefit you and others.

## Matrices: Putting It All Together

- By organizing, defining, and placing your clear, actionable behaviors, routines, habits, and rituals into a performance matrix, you can take greater control of your goals and intentions. Your preparation, pre-performance, during-performance, and post-performance phases are not just steps but powerful tools that you can use to consistently perform and own your confidence. Consistent, deliberate, focused action on your identities, the six fundamentals of a healthy performer, and your Core Four (plus one) mental skills is not just a process, but an adventure in empowerment that increases and compounds your confidence. Without having a plan, we remain stuck in theory. Putting behavior changes consistently into action, not just when you feel like it, will teach you about what works for you.

- Using a performance matrix allows you to practice, reflect, iteratively improve or overhaul, and then recommit. To perform sustainably at your best levels over time, it's not just about hoping for the best, but rather requires you to take an active role in the process. The hard part is maintaining the consistency over time to stick to your plan and make adjustments as needed, especially when you don't feel like it. Improvement is like a seed planted in the ground; it needs time, patience, water, sunlight, and love.

- See the link in the appendix to download blank or completed performance matrices. The completed ones include an overall performance and health matrix and a matrix for your mental game. The concepts used in these matrices come from my experiences, data from scientific studies, and tools that other professionals have used which have proven effective. The matrices provide a solid framework for starting small and implementing gradual improvements in each phase (preparation, pre-performance, during performance, and post-performance). Having a simple, executable plan is better than a complex, non-executed one.

# SECTION 7

## Systems

# Chapter 16

# Helping Others Win (HOW)

A system is defined by Dictionary.com as being "an assemblage or combination of things or parts forming a complex or unitary whole." I see a system as a dynamic, complex whole where interrelated and interdependent parts create something greater than the sum of those parts. It's also important to note that the nature of systems is complex and dynamic. For example, when a spider web vibrates in one area, the ripple across the whole system alerts the spider of a change. Because of a system's dynamic and interrelated nature, changes in one part can shift the entire system and vice versa.

The power of systems lies in their potential for synergy and synchronicity. When a system optimizes its parts and eliminates unnecessary friction between them, it operates more smoothly and effectively. An optimized system can produce results far greater than the sum of its parts because the equation becomes exponential, not additive. Like a well-oiled machine, goals are far more likely to be achieved, if not surpassed, when a frictionless system is in harmony and works more efficiently and effectively. A system is optimized when each healthy part synergistically works together with and responds to the other parts.

This concept of optimization applies across all types of systems, regardless of size or type. Systems can be as small as a cellular organism or as large as the multiverse. Types of human systems include families, businesses, schools, organizations and communities, and athletic departments. A team is a type of system, and the confident performer model is a system within the system. Imagine the synergistic power of every parent, athlete, coach, and TAT member within the PACT system being optimized such that the team becomes a consistently powerful force with which few can reckon.

## Common Goal

Teams are formed to achieve a common goal that an individual cannot achieve alone. If a quarterback could beat another football team alone, why would they play with teammates? Of course, an individual athlete would not get far on any down on the football field if one player was competing against 11. A quarterback needs their teammates to play their roles and execute their assignments so they can all have a chance at beating the other team.

Each part of the system plays a different role in helping the team achieve that common goal, and each part uniquely contributes to that achievement. It's fairly universally agreed-upon that a positive sporting experience is the foundational common goal of sporting systems, no matter the level of pressure, skill, or experience. If the experience is positive, everyone is more likely to make the effort and investment of putting in the hard work required. Even at the pro level, where earnings can be extraordinary, the athlete will not last long if every part of their experience is miserable. Regardless of the financial incentives of professional sports, the hard parts of athletic experiences can be tolerated and persevered through when there are enough positive reasons to continue to stay engaged.

Most parents would never intentionally register their children for a sporting experience that is miserable, degrading, or lackluster. Coaches would not sign up to continue to coach if their mental, physical, and spiritual state took a beating with there being no ultimate reward or life satisfaction. An athlete would not stay in their sport if the experience was worthless, ugly, or painful, and without a hint of fun or something positive to gain. The TAT members would move on to other positions if being involved in sports was nothing but miserable. Many sports evolved from military and war preparation to being activities for leisure and fun. When parents, athletes, and coaches agree about what they want to accomplish, they are far more likely to work with one another rather than against each other. To have role clarity and perform well, everyone must agree on the common goal and have a clear understanding of their responsibilities in that role and what is not their roles' responsibilities. The common goal is a positive sporting experience for all and the by-product of self-mastery for everyone is winning more games and championships. When winning is the only focus, more problems tend to arise with more blaming, shaming and complaining.

This clarity lays the groundwork for true teamwork. When group members agree on their goals, maintain clarity of roles, and commit to fulfilling their roles to their utmost ability, only then do they become a genuine team. Otherwise, they are just a group of people. Agreements, acceptance, and commitments give the system and the team a chance to win more games and achieve the common goal of having a positive sporting experience. This shared commitment and understanding can unite a team, making them stronger, more trusting, and more cohesive.

The winning systems approach starts with a commonly agreed-upon goal that each role commits to helping the system achieve. Then, when the people in each role understand, accept, and commit to playing their part and fulfilling their responsibilities while not trying to do someone else's job, the frictionless system has a chance to meet or exceed goals and expectations. Winning Systems is an approach where truly everyone wins over a lifetime because they gain self-mastery while contributing to the whole and learning how to win. This system not only leads to victories on the field but also fosters personal growth and self-mastery, empowering each individual within the system.

## Be a Force for Good

As Sir Richard Branson has said, "Business should be a force for good." Athletics should be a force for good also, and athletes can use sports as the ultimate training ground for becoming a force for good. An excellent example of an athlete becoming a force for good is Lionel Messi, considered to be the GOAT of football (soccer). Messi has partnered with organizations that focus on conservation efforts to protect animal species and habitats and uses his global social platform to spread the message about this work while impressing the world with his skill and tenacity.

Many sports organizations, public figures and celebrities, and regular people like me have aligned themselves with the United Nations 17 Sustainable Development Goals (SDGs). I have joined forces with other entrepreneurs to dedicate one percent of my effort, materials, and profits to benefit organizations that are working toward achieving the SDGs. The World Athletics organization aligns its efforts with 13 of the 17 goals and encourages athletes to live planet-friendly lifestyles.

Having a big-picture focus on becoming a force for good can encourage a helpful perspective shift from the narrow focus of a disappointing performance or loss. Learn from the loss and move on, keeping the big picture in mind. If you commit to being a force for good on this planet, you are already doing a great job in life! Using athletics as the training ground to learn how to own your confidence enhances being a force for good. The skill of maintaining both a big-picture and a narrow focus helps you keep your competition in perspective and win the game of life.

# Chapter 17

# Reflection

*Carpe diem; carpe punctum.* The present moment is the only time we truly have to make a difference. No matter how much we wish the past were different, it's beyond our control, and the only thing we can change is the story we tell ourselves about it. If you consider that the events of the past happened for you, not to you, how would that change your perspective and shape your future?

But knowing the power of the present and actually living it are two very different things. I have spent most of my life on a fast train, running and gunning to get to the next destination, and I missed enjoying the proverbial beautiful scenery along the way. I wanted so badly to get away from the present moment and into the future that when I arrived at whatever destination I thought would bring me happiness, peace, contentment, joy, and freedom, I realized I was mistaken.

So what comes next, and what is "now"? This moment-to-moment dynamic opportunity is designed to be seized. *Carpe punctum* means to seize and savor the moment instead of running away from it toward the next thing. It's about slowing down and being more thoughtful and engaged, and experiencing the real destination of happiness, contentment, satisfaction, joy, and freedom in the present moment. Smile, breathe, and remember that everything is and will be okay. Go and live the better to best version of your multiple selves by owning your confidence and pursuing the mastery of your Self, giving the world all that you've got.

# Appendix A

# Sample PACT Agreement

A copy of this agreement can also be downloaded at www.DrAndreaWieland. com/Resources

Name of the Team _____

Name of the PACT Member _____

Role in the PACT (circle one): Parent     Athlete          Coach   TAT

In my role as a PACT member, I commit to:

- Understanding the full extent of my role in this winning system and playing my role to the best of my ability, even when I am having a bad day. Part of my role is to have the best attitude I can, and I am 100 percent responsible for my attitude, effort, and focus.
- Learning about the other roles in the PACT and how they contribute to our whole. I understand that I need to play only my role and not anyone else's.
- Doubling-down on my commitment to play my role well, especially when I'm stressed and frustrated.
- Being an exemplar of good sportsmanship and showing respect for all players, coaches, parents, and the TAT.

- Showing respect for my sport, the umpires, judges or referees, my opponents or competition, and the spectators.
- Listening to and following important information for the benefit of our winning system.
- Asking questions respectfully if I do not understand or disagree with a decision.
- Having patience with myself and others, staying curious, and having a sense of humor, even when adversity arises.
- Our common goal of having a positive sporting experience for our PACT and remembering that sports are supposed to be fun.

If I am a parent, I understand that athletes are expected to attend all practices, games, and tournaments unless absences are communicated ahead of time and only under very rare circumstances. Part of my commitment means scheduling appointments, vacations, or other events outside of the season.

Any athlete over the age of 14 is expected to communicate with the head coach regarding being absent for any reason unless the athlete is incapacitated and unable to do so.

As a member of this PACT, I understand that coaches make the decisions regarding who starts, the lineups, substitutes, and how much playing time is given. I accept that all players won't play the same amount.

As a parent(s), I/we fully understand and have discussed with our child the agreements we are making as members of this PACT.

PARENT

_____ Mother's/Guardian's Signature and Date

_____ (Print Name)

_____ Father's/Guardian's Signature and Date

_____ (Print Name)

ATHLETE

_____ Athlete Signature and Date

_____ (Print Name)

COACH

_____ Head Coach Signature and Date

_____ Print Name)

TAT

_____ TAT Member Signature and Date

_____ (Print Name)

# Appendix B

# Recommended Tools

## Chapter 3:

The Winning Systems Psychology, PC program offers coaching, webinars, online courses, in-person seminars, and mental training camps. You can learn more at www.drandreawieland.com.

## Chapter 6:

The MBTI or CPI are two assessments that can help you understand your personality type and tendencies. You can take a free MBTI assessment online at www.16personalities.com

The IFS-Institute offers levels 1-3 trainings for professionals interested in using IFS in their practice. I recommend reading or listening to any of the book offerings. There are books available for children and those working with children. The books I recommend for non-practitioners are (1) *No Bad Parts* by Richard Schwartz and (2) *You Are the One You've Been Waiting For* by Richard Schwartz.

## Chapter 10:

I encourage you to take the free Saboteurs assessment at www.positiveintelligence.com/saboteurs

## Chapter 12:

Heroic's 10-month coaching course has reached thousands of people in almost 200 countries. Heroic.us offers an incredible app for setting daily identities, selecting your virtues, and targeting behavior. To try the app for free for one year, go to www.bit.ly/HeroicAW. This site will take you to my page. The app setup page will ask for a credit card, and one year later you will be charged for the upcoming year, so don't forget to set a cancelation date if you don't want to continue with the app. You can also sign up for Heroic Coaching and Heroic Workshop Instructor training through the same bit.ly link.

I use the Heroic app consistently to get a 'Soul Force' score of 101, which as a key feature of the app is a measure of your alignment with your chosen Choice Identities. I have a daily commitment to maintain my streak and persist in my values and targeted actions to live and express my better to best self. This app has been my best investment in personal and mental performance development, and I hope you find it to be as incredibly useful and game changing as I have. If anything changes with this offer, please look for updates on my website, www.drandreawieland.com, or send me an email: andrea@drandreawieland.com

Brian Johnson, the founder and CEO of Heroic Public Benefit Corporation and the creator of the Heroic app, has also distilled over 750 books into a collection of reviews that he calls Philosopher's Notes. He has created more than 50 courses on the top personal development constructs, such as motivation, goals, confidence, sleep, and nutrition, and over 1,900 plus ones where he discusses a power-punch tool or concept in a one- to two-minute video. This wealth of resources is available to guide and support you in your personal development adventure. I suggest taking a look at his website at www.heroic.us.

## Chapter 13:

One of my best friends and former teammates, Kris (Fillat) Buchanan developed the GOODONYA Organic Hydration product, which is an organic daily electrolyte and mineral supplement to add to your water. You can learn more about the product and order it at www.goodonyaorganic.com.

I also recommend a supplement called Juice Plus+, which is made of dried compounded fruits and vegetables in a capsule form, and is backed by over 40 published clinical research studies. You can learn more about the product and order it at www.andreawieland.juiceplus.com

I have taken this supplement daily for over 15 years, and it gives me peace of mind that I am putting empirically evidenced clean nutrients into my body to support my whole self and athletic performance at the cellular level.

## Chapter 14:

The Short Moments community offers four basic responses to data, which can be accessed at www.shortmoments.com

## Chapter 15:

To request and download an example performance matrix plan and worksheet to build your own, go to www.drandreawieland.com/resources.

# Appendix C

# References

Anderson, Lydia, Chanell Washington, Rose M. Kreider, and Thomas Gryn. 2023. "Share of One-Person Households More Than Tripled from 1940 to 2020." *United States Census Bureau*, June 8, 2023. https://www.census.gov/library/stories/2023/06/more-than-a-quarter-all-households-have-one-person.html.

Balanced View Team. Short Moments, Many Times: Open Intelligence Becomes Obvious!: The Most Powerful and Easy Way to Live. Balanced View, 2012.

Bandura, Albert. *Social Foundations of Thought and Action: A Social Cognitive Theory.* Englewood Cliffs, NJ: Prentice-Hall, 1985.

Bassham, Lanny. *With Winning in Mind.* 3rd ed. Mental Management Systems, 2011.

Bassham, L. *Parenting Champions:* What Every Parent Should Know about The Mental Game. Mental Management Systems, 2017.

Bleidorn, Wiebke, Ted Schwaba, Anqing Zheng, Christopher J. Hopwood, Susana S. Sosa, Brent W. Roberts, and Daniel A. Briley. "Personality Stability and Change: A Meta-Analysis of Longitudinal Studies." Psychological Bulletin 148, no. 7–8 (2022): 588–619.

Bouchard, Thomas J., Jr., David T. Lykken, Matt McGue, Nancy L. Segal, and Auke Tellegen. "Sources of Human Psychological Differences: The Minnesota Study of Twins Reared Apart." Science 250, no. 4978 (1990): 223–28, https://doi.org/10.1126/science.2218526.

Brown, Richard P., and Patricia L. Gerbarg. The Healing Power of the Breath: Simple Techniques to Reduce Stress and Anxiety, Enhance Concentration, and Balance Your Emotions. Shambhala Publications, 2012.

Brown, Nicholas J. L., Alan D. Sokal, and Harris L. Friedman. "The Complex Dynamics of Wishful Thinking: The Critical Positivity Ratio." American Psychologist 68, no. 9 (2013): 801–13, https://doi.org/10.1037/a0032850.

Chamine, Shirzad. Positive Intelligence: Why Only 20% of Teams and Individuals Achieve Their True Potential and How You Can Achieve Yours. Greenleaf Book Group Press, 2012.

Collins, James C., and Jerry I. Porras. Built to Last: Successful Habits of Visionary Companies. Harper Business Essentials, 2002.

Costa, Paul T., Jr., and Robert R. McCrae. "The Revised NEO Personality Inventory (NEO-PI-R)." In The SAGE Handbook of Personality Theory and Assessment, Vol. 2: Personality Measurement and Testing, edited by Gregory J. Boyle, Gerald Matthews, and Donald H. Saklofske, 179–198. Sage Publications, 2008.

Divine, Mark. Unbeatable Mind: Forge Resiliency and Mental Toughness to Succeed at an Elite Level. 3rd ed. CreateSpace Independent Publishing Platform, 2012.

Dweck, Carol. Mindset: The New Psychology of Success. Random House, 2006.

Fredrickson, Barbara L. Positivity: Groundbreaking Research Reveals How to Embrace the Hidden Strength of Positive Emotions, Overcome Negativity, and Thrive. New York: Crown Archetype, 2009.

Fredrickson, Barbara L., and Marcial F. Losada. "Positive Affect and the Complex Dynamics of Human Flourishing." American Psychologist 60, no. 7 (2005): 678–86, https://doi.org/10.1037/0003-066X.60.7.678.

Gaur, Deepika. and Sandhya Gupta. "The Impact of Parental Support on Adolescent's Emotional Intelligence and Self-Esteem: A Comprehensive Literature Review." International Journal of Psychology Research 6, no. 1 (2024): 65–68. https://doi.org/10.33545/26648903.2024.v6.i1b.51.

Gould, Daniel, Kristen Dieffenbach, and Aaron Moffett. "Psychological Characteristics and Their Development in Olympic Champions." Journal of Applied Sport Psychology 14, no. 3 (2002): 172–204, https://www.doi.org/10.1080/10413200290103482.

Green, Kristophe, and Dacher Keltner. "What Happens When We Reconnect With Nature." Greater Good Magazine, March 2017. https://greatergood.berkeley.edu/article/item/what_happens_when_we_reconnect_with_nature.

Gupta, P., M. Galimberti, Y. Liu, S. Beck, A. Wingo, T. Wingo, K. Adhikari, H. R. Kranzler, VA Million Veteran Program, M. B. Stein, J. Gelernter, and D. F. Levey. "A Genome-Wide Investigation into the Underlying Genetic Architecture of Personality Traits and Overlap with Psychopathology." Nature Human Behaviour 8, no. 11 (2024): 2235–49.

Hatton, I. A., E. D. Galbraith, N. S. C. Merleau, T. P. Miettinen, B. M. D. Smith, and J. A. Shander. "The Human Cell Count and Size Distribution." Proceedings of the National Academy of Sciences of the United States of America 120, no. 39 (2023): 1–1, https://doi.org/10.1073/PNAS.2303077120.

Hays, Pamela A. "Addressing the Complexities of Culture and Gender in Counseling." Journal of Counseling & Development 74, no. 4 (1996): 332–38, https://www.doi.org/10.1002/j.1556-6676.1996.tb01876.x.

Hays, Pamela A. Addressing Cultural Complexities in Practice: Assessment, Diagnosis, and Therapy. 2nd ed. Washington, DC: American Psychological Association, 2007.

Hof, Wim, and Elissa Epel. The Wim Hof Method: Activate Your Full Human Potential. Louisville, CO: Sounds True, 2020.

James, William. The Principles of Psychology. New York: Henry Holt and Company, 1890.

Johnson, Brian. Arete: Activate Your Heroic Potential. Heroic Blackstone, 2023.

Jung, C. G. Collected Works of C. G. Jung, Volume 6: Psychological Types. Princeton University Press, 1921.

Karpman, Stephen. "Fairy Tales and Script Drama Analysis." Transactional Analysis Bulletin 7, no. 28 (1968): 53–57.

Katie, Byron. *Loving What Is: How to Transform Your Life by Applying the Four Questions.* Penguin Random House, 2003.

Kerr, James. Legacy: What the All Blacks Can Teach Us About the Business of Life. London: Constable & Robinson, 2013.

Kornfield, Jack. No Time like the Present: Finding Freedom, Love, and Joy Right Where You Are. New York: Atria Books, 2017.

Lee, Al, and Don Campbell. Perfect Breathing: Transform Your Life One Breath at a Time. San Francisco: Chronicle Books, 2013.

Li, Qing. Forest Bathing: How Trees Help You Find Health and Happiness. New York: Macmillan, 2014.

Maslow, Abraham H. "A Theory of Human Motivation." Psychological Review 50, no. 4

(1943): 370–96, https://doi.org/10.1037/h0054346.

McChesney, Chris, Sean Covey, and Jim Huling. The 4 Disciplines of Execution: Achieving

Your Wildly Important Goals. New York: Free Press, 2012.

McKeown, Patrick. The Oxygen Advantage: The Simple, Scientifically Proven Breathing Techniques for a Healthier, Slimmer, Faster, and Fitter You. New York: William Morrow, an imprint of HarperCollins Publishers, 2015.

McLellan, M., S. Allahabadi, and N. Pandya. "Youth Sports Specialization and Its Effect on Professional, Elite, and Olympic Athlete Performance, Career Longevity, and Injury Rates." The Orthopaedic Journal of Sports Medicine 10, no. 11 (2022), https://www.doi.org/10.1177/23259671221129594.

Mustile, M., D. Kourtis, M. G. Edwards, D. I. Donaldson, and M. Ietswaart. "Neural Correlates of Motor Imagery and Execution in Real-World Dynamic Behavior: Evidence for Similarities and Differences." Frontiers in Human Neuroscience 18 (2024): 1412307. https://doi.org/10.3389/fnhum.2024.1412307.

Myers, Isabel Briggs, and Mary H. McCaulley. Manual: A Guide to the Development and Use of the Myers-Briggs Type Indicator. Palo Alto, CA: Consulting Psychologists Press, 1985.

Nestor, James. Breath: The New Science of a Lost Art. New York: Penguin Life, 2020.

Oettingen, Gabriele. Rethinking Positive Thinking: Inside the New Science of Motivation. New York: Ballantine Books, 2014.

Olsson, Anders. Conscious Breathing: Discover the Power of Your Breath. Self-published, 2012.

Randall, Ken, Mary Isaacson, and Carrie Ciro. "Validity and Reliability of the Myers-Briggs Personality Type Indicator: A Systematic Review and Meta-Analysis." Journal of Best Practices in Health Professions Diversity 10 (2017): 1–27.

Ranehill, Eva, Anna Dreber, Magnus Johannesson, Susanne Leiberg, Sunhae Sul, and Roberto A. Weber. "Assessing the Robustness of Power Posing: No Effect on Hormones and Risk Tolerance in a Large Sample of Men and Women." Psychological Science 26, no. 5 (2015): 653–56. https://doi.org/10.1177/0956797614553946.

Robbins, Mel. The 5 Second Rule: Transform Your Life, Work, and Confidence with Everyday Courage. New York: Savio Republic, 2017.

Schwartz, Richard C. Internal Family Systems Therapy. New York: Guilford Press, 1985.

Taylor, Andrea Faber, and Frances E. Kuo. "Could Exposure to Everyday Green Spaces Help Treat ADHD? Evidence from Children's Play Settings." Applied Psychology: Health and Well-Being 3, no. 3 (2011): 281–303, https://doi.org/10.1111/j.1758-0854.2011.01052.x.

Tseng, Jessica, and Jordan Poppenk. "Brain Meta-State Transitions Demarcate Thoughts Across Task Contexts, Exposing the Mental Noise of Trait Neuroticism." Nature Communications 11 (2020): 3480. https://doi.org/10.1038/s41467-020-17255-9.

van den Berg, Maartje M. H. E., Jolanda Maas, Remy Muller, Anja Braun, Wendy Kaandorp, Reinoud van Lien, Margo N. van Poppel, Willem van Mechelen, and Agnes E. van den Berg. "Autonomic Nervous System Responses to Viewing Green and Built Settings: Differentiating Between Sympathetic and Parasympathetic Activity." International Journal of Environmental Research and Public Health 12, no. 12 (2015): 15860–74, https://doi.org/10.3390/ijerph121215026.

Vranich, Belisa, and Brian Sabin. Breathing for Warriors: Master Your Breath to Unlock More Strength, Greater Endurance, Sharper Precision, Faster Recovery, and an Unshakable Inner Game. New York: Simon & Schuster, 2020.

Young, Chris. "Green Peace." *Greater Good Magazine*, September 1, 2004. https://greatergood.berkeley.edu/article/item/green_p.

Weil, Andrew. Eight Weeks to Optimum Health: A Proven Program for Taking Full Advantage of Your Body's Natural Healing Power. New York: Ballantine Books, 2007.

# Endnotes

1    Stephen Karpman, "Fairy Tales and Script Drama Analysis," *Transactional Analysis Bulletin* 7, no. 28 (1968): 53–57.

2    James Kerr, *Legacy: What the All Blacks Can Teach Us About the Business of Life* (Constable & Robinson, 2013).

3    Daniel Gould, Kristen Dieffenbach, and Aaron Moffett, "Psychological Characteristics and Their Development in Olympic Champions," *Journal of Applied Sport Psychology* 14, no. 3 (2002): 172–204, https://www.doi.org/10.1080/10413200290103482.

4    Albert Bandura, Social Foundations of Thought and Action: A Social Cognitive Theory Englewood Cliffs, NJ: Prentice-Hall, 1986).

5    Lanny Bassham, *With Winning in Mind* (Mental Management Systems, 2011).

6    Deepika Gaur and Sandhya Gupta. "The Impact of Parental Support on Adolescent's Emotional Intelligence and Self-Esteem: A Comprehensive Literature Review," *International Journal of Psychology Research* 6, no. 1 (2024): 65–68.

7    Brian Johnson, Arete: Activate Your Heroic Potential (Heroic Blackstone, 2023).

8    Carol Dweck, *Mindset: The New Psychology of Success* (Random House, 2006).

9    Lanny Bassham, *Parenting Champions: What Every Parent Should Know about The Mental Game* (Mental Management Systems, 2017).

10   Maddison McLellan, Sachin Allahabadi, and Nirav K. Pandya, "Youth Sports Specialization and Its Effect on Professional, Elite, and Olympic Athlete Performance, Career Longevity, and Injury Rates," *The Orthopaedic Journal of Sports Medicine* 10, no. 11 (2022), https://www.doi.org/10.1177/23259671221129594.

11   Abraham H. Maslow, "A Theory of Human Motivation," *Psychological Review* 50, no. 4 (1943): 370–96, https://doi.org/10.1037/h0054346.

12   Pamela A. Hays, "Addressing the Complexities of Culture and Gender in Counseling," *Journal of Counseling & Development* 74, no. 4 (1996): 332–338, https://www.doi.org/10.1002/j.1556-6676.1996.tb01876.x.

13   Shirzad Chamine, *Positive Intelligence: Why Only 20% of Teams and Individuals Achieve Their True Potential and How You Can Achieve Yours* (Greenleaf Book Group Press, 2012).

14   William James, *The Principles of Psychology* (Henry Holt and Company, 1890).

15   Wiebke Bleidorn, Ted Schwaba, Anqing Zheng, Christopher J. Hopwood, Susana S. Sosa, Brent W. Roberts, and Daniel A. Briley, "Personality Stability and Change: A Meta-Analysis of Longitudinal Studies," *Psychological Bulletin* 148, no. 7–8 (2022): 588–619.

16  Thomas J. Bouchard Jr., David T. Lykken, Matt McGue, Nancy L. Segal, and Auke Tellegen, "Sources of Human Psychological Differences: The Minnesota Study of Twins Reared Apart," *Science* 250, no. 4978 (1990): 223–28, https://doi.org/10.1126/science.2218526.

17  Paul T. Costa Jr. and Robert R. McCrae, "The Revised NEO Personality Inventory (NEO-PI-R)," in *The SAGE Handbook of Personality Theory and Assessment* (Sage Publications, 2008).

18  P. Gupta, M. Galimberti, Y. Liu, S. Beck, A. Wingo, T. Wingo, K. Adhikari, H. R. Kranzler, VA Million Veteran Program, M. B. Stein, J. Gelernter, and D. F. Levey, "A Genome-Wide Investigation into the Underlying Genetic Architecture of Personality Traits and Overlap with Psychopathology," Nature Human Behaviour 8, no. 11 (2024): 2235–49.

19  Richard C. Schwartz, *Internal Family Systems Therapy* (Guilford Press, 1985).

20  Isabel Briggs Myers and Mary H. McCaulley, *Manual: A Guide to the Development and Use of the Myers-Briggs Type Indicator* (Consulting Psychologists Press, 1985).

21  Ken Randall, Mary Isaacson, and Carrie Ciro. "Validity and Reliability of the Myers-Briggs Personality Type Indicator: A Systematic Review and Meta-Analysis." *Journal of Best Practices in Health Professions Diversity* 10 (2017): 1–27.

22  Pamela A. Hays, *Addressing Cultural Complexities in Practice: Assessment, Diagnosis, and Therapy* (American Psychological Association, 2007).

23  Carl G. Jung, *Collected Works of C. G. Jung, Volume 6: Psychological Types* (Princeton University Press, 1921).

24  Shirzad Chamine, Positive Intelligence: *Why Only 20% of Teams and Individuals Achieve Their True Potential and How You Can Achieve Yours* (Austin, TX: Greenleaf Book Group Press, 2012).

25  Chris McChesney, Sean Covey, and Jim Huling, *The 4 Disciplines of Execution: Achieving Your Wildly Important Goals* (Free Press, 2012).

26  James C. Collins and Jerry I. Porras. *Built to Last: Successful Habits of Visionary Companies* (Harper Business Essentials, 2002).

27  Gabriele Oettingen, *Rethinking Positive Thinking: Inside the New Science of Motivation* (Ballantine Books, 2014).

28  Mark Divine, *Unbeatable Mind: Forge Resiliency and Mental Toughness to Succeed at an Elite Level* (CreateSpace Independent Publishing Platform, 2012).

29  Mel Robbins, *The 5 Second Rule: Transform Your Life, Work, and Confidence with Everyday Courage* (Savio Republic, 2017).

30  Andrew Weil, *Eight Weeks to Optimum Health: A Proven Program for Taking Full Advantage of Your Body's Natural Healing Power* (Ballantine Books, 2007).

31  Patrick McKeown, *The Oxygen Advantage: The Simple, Scientifically Proven Breathing Techniques for a Healthier, Slimmer, Faster, and Fitter You* (HarperCollins Publishers, 2015).

32  Ian A. Hatton, Eric D. Galbraith, Nono S. C. Merleau, Teemu P. Miettinen, Benjamin McDonald Smith, and Jeffery A. Shander, "The Human Cell Count and Size Distribution," *Proceedings of the National Academy of Sciences of the United States of America* 120, no. 39 (2023): 1–1, https://doi.org/10.1073/PNAS.2303077120.

33  Kristophe Green and Dacher Keltner, "What Happens When We Reconnect with Nature," *Greater Good Magazine*, March 1, 2017. https://greatergood.berkeley.edu/article/item/what_happens_when_we_reconnect_with_nature.

34  Qing Li, *Forest Bathing: How Trees Help You Find Health and Happiness* (Macmillan, 2014).

35  Lydia Anderson, Chanell Washington, Rose M. Kreider, and Thomas Gryn, "Share of One-Person Households More Than Tripled from 1940 to 2020," *United States Census Bureau*, June 8, 2023, https://www.census.gov/library/stories/2023/06/more-than-a-quarter-all-households-have-one-person.html.

36  Magdalena MHE van den Berg, Jolanda Maas, Remy Muller, Anja Braun, Wendy Kaandorp, Reinoud van Lien, Margo N. van Poppel, Willem van Mechelen, and Agnes E. van den Berg, "Autonomic Nervous System Responses to Viewing Green and Built Settings: Differentiating Between Sympathetic and Parasympathetic Activity," *International Journal of Environmental Research and Public Health* 12, no. 12 (2015): 15860–74, https://doi.org/10.3390/ijerph121215026.

37  Chris Young, "Green Peace," *Greater Good Magazine*, September 1, 2004. https://greatergood.berkeley.edu/article/item/green_p.

38  Andrea Faber Taylor and Frances E. Kuo, "Could Exposure to Everyday Green Spaces Help Treat ADHD? Evidence from Children's Play Settings" *Applied Psychology: Health and Well-Being* 3, no. 3 (2011): 281–303, https://doi.org/10.1111/j.1758-0854.2011.01052.x.

39  Jack Kornfield, *No Time like the Present: Finding Freedom, Love, and Joy Right Where You Are* (Atria Books, 2017).

40  James Nestor, *Breath: The New Science of a Lost Art* (Penguin Life, 2020).

41  Anders Olsson, *Conscious Breathing: Discover the Power of Your Breath* (Self-published, 2012).

42  Belisa Vranich and Brian Sabin, *Breathing for Warriors: Master Your Breath to Unlock More Strength, Greater Endurance, Sharper Precision, Faster Recovery, and an Unshakable Inner Game* (Simon & Schuster, 2020).

43  Richard P. Brown and Patricia L. Gerbarg, *The Healing Power of the Breath: Simple Techniques to Reduce Stress and Anxiety, Enhance Concentration, and Balance Your Emotions* (Shambhala Publications, 2012).

44  Al Lee and Don Campbell, *Perfect Breathing: Transform Your Life One Breath at a Time* (Chronicle Books, 2013).

45  Wim Hof and Elissa Epel, *The Wim Hof Method: Activate Your Full Human Potential* (Sounds True, 2020).

46  Jessica Tseng and Jordan Poppenk, "Brain Meta-State Transitions Demarcate Thoughts Across Task Contexts, Exposing the Mental Noise of Trait Neuroticism," *Nature Communications* 11 (2020): 3480, https://doi.org/10.1038/s41467-020-17255-9.

47  Byron Katie and Stephen Mitchell, Loving What Is: Four Questions That Can Change Your Life (New York: Harmony Books, 2002), 3.

48  Short Moments Team, *Short Moments, Many Times: Open Intelligence Becomes Obvious!: The Most Powerful and Easy Way to Live.* (Balanced View, 2012).

49  Eva Ranehill, Anna Dreber, Magnus Johannesson, Susanne Leiberg, Sunhae Sul, and Roberto A. Weber, "Assessing the Robustness of Power Posing: No Effect on Hormones and Risk Tolerance in a Large Sample of Men and Women," *Psychological Science* 26, no. 5 (2015): 653–56, https://doi.org/10.1177/0956797614553946.

50  Magda Mustile, Dimitrios Kourtis, Martin G. Edwards, David I. Donaldson, and Mag-

dalena Ietswaart, "Neural Correlates of Motor Imagery and Execution in Real-World Dynamic Behavior: Evidence for Similarities and Differences," *Frontiers in Human Neuroscience* 18 (2024): 1412307, https://doi.org/10.3389/fnhum.2024.1412307.

51   Neal Brennan, Blocks, podcast, accessed May 2025, https://podcasts.apple.com/us/podcast/blocks-w-neal-brennan/id1658660161.

52   Barbara L Fredrickson, *Positivity: Groundbreaking Research Reveals How to Embrace the Hidden Strength of Positive Emotions, Overcome Negativity, and Thrive* (Crown Archetype, 2009).

53   Barbara L. Fredrickson and Marcial F. Losada, "Positive Affect and the Complex Dynamics of Human Flourishing," *American Psychologist* 60, no. 7 (2005): 678–86, https://doi.org/10.1037/0003-066X.60.7.678.

54   Nicholas J. L. Brown, Alan D. Sokal, and Harris L. Friedman, "The Complex Dynamics of Wishful Thinking: The Critical Positivity Ratio," *American Psychologist* 68, no. 9 (2013): 801–13, https://doi.org/10.1037/a0032850.

www.ingramcontent.com/pod-product-compliance
Lightning Source LLC
Chambersburg PA
CBHW071415090426
42737CB00011B/1476